Sustaining Key Skills in the UK Naval Industry

T0302678

Hans Pung • Laurence Smallman • Mark V. Arena • James G. Kallimani
Gordon T. Lee • Samir Puri • John F. Schank

Prepared for the UK Ministry of Defence

Approved for public release;
distribution unlimited

RAND EUROPE

This research was sponsored by the Ministry of Defence and conducted within RAND Europe and the International Security and Defense Policy Center of the RAND National Security Research Division.

Library of Congress Cataloging-in-Publication Data

Sustaining key skills in the UK naval industry / Hans Pung ... [et al.].
p. cm.
Includes bibliographical references.
ISBN 978-0-8330-4410-5 (pbk. : alk. paper)
1. Shipbuilding industry—Employees—Great Britain. 2. Engineering personnel—Great Britain. 3. Warships—Great Britain—Design and construction. 4. Submarines (Ships)—Great Britain—Design and construction. 5. Great Britain. Ministry of Defence—Procurement. I. Pung, Hans.

VM299.7.G7S87 2008
331.7'6238250941—dc22

2008005601

The RAND Corporation is a nonprofit research organization providing objective analysis and effective solutions that address the challenges facing the public and private sectors around the world. RAND's publications do not necessarily reflect the opinions of its research clients and sponsors.

Published 2008 by the RAND Corporation
1776 Main Street, P.O. Box 2138, Santa Monica, CA 90407-2138
1200 South Hayes Street, Arlington, VA 22202-5050
4570 Fifth Avenue, Suite 600, Pittsburgh, PA 15213-2665
RAND URL: http://www.rand.org/
To order RAND documents or to obtain additional information, contact
Distribution Services: Telephone: (310) 451-7002;
Fax: (310) 451-6915; Email: order@rand.org

Preface

The United Kingdom's Ministry of Defence (MOD) is pursuing several shipbuilding programmes—including the *Astute* submarine class, the Future Aircraft Carrier (CVF), the Future Surface Combatant (FSC), Military Afloat Reach and Sustainability (MARS) vessels, and the Type 45 destroyer—that will potentially stress the UK's domestic shipbuilding industry capacity over the next 15 years.

In 2005, RAND published an examination of this issue, *The United Kingdom's Naval Shipbuilding Industrial Base: The Next Fifteen Years*,[1] which has been widely cited in government and press circles in the United Kingdom and was referenced by MOD in the maritime section of its recently released Defence Industrial Strategy (DIS).[2]

Since the release of the RAND study and the DIS, MOD has identified a series of new but related questions connected with that original work. Those questions focus on the need for, and retention of, specific technical skills in the UK's maritime industry.

As a result, in 2006, MOD asked RAND to undertake a follow-on study using a similar but expanded analytical approach to help it better understand how to sustain technical skills in the maritime sector. In particular, MOD was interested in exploring the relationship between the demand created by its ship and submarine acquisition pro-

---

1 Mark V. Arena, Hans Pung, Cynthia R. Cook, Jefferson P. Marquis, Jessie Riposo, and Gordon T. Lee, *The United Kingdom's Naval Shipbuilding Industrial Base: The Next Fifteen Years*, Santa Monica, Calif.: RAND Corporation, MG-294-MOD, 2005.

2 UK Ministry of Defence, *Defence Industrial Strategy*, Defence White Paper CM 6697, December 2005.

gramme and the supply of the technical workforce needed to support that programme.

RAND analysed these issues between 2006 and mid-2007, employing both qualitative and quantitative methodologies. This monograph describes the analytical procedures that the RAND team followed and summarises its findings and recommendations. The results indicate that the supply-demand relationship is highly complex and that some technical skills are extremely sensitive to demand.

As part of this project, RAND provided MOD with management tools that allowed it to model these dynamic relationships and assess options for sustaining these skills.

This research should be of interest to MOD's Defence Equipment and Support organisation, as well as to service and defence managers and policymakers involved in weapon system acquisition on both sides of the Atlantic. It should also be of interest to shipbuilding industry executives in the United Kingdom.

This research was sponsored by the Ministry of Defence and conducted within RAND Europe and the International Security and Defense Policy Center of the RAND National Security Research Division (NSRD).

For more information on RAND Europe, contact the Director of its Defence and Security Programme, Hans Pung. He can be reached by email at Hans_Pung@rand.org; by phone at +44 1223 353 329; or by mail at RAND Europe, Westbrook Centre, Milton Road, Cambridge, CB4 1YG, United Kingdom.

For more information on RAND's International Security and Defense Policy Center, contact the Director, James Dobbins. He can be reached by email at James_Dobbins@rand.org; by phone at 703-413-1100 extension 5134; or by mail at RAND, 1200 South Hayes Street, Arlington, Virginia 22202-5050. More information about RAND is available at www.rand.org.

Contents

Figures

Tables

Summary

To preserve its ability to design, build, and support complex warships and submarines, the UK Ministry of Defence (MOD) will need to preserve and sustain several key technical skills in the maritime domain. In particular, it needs to nurture detailed designers and professional engineers involved in various stages of surface ship and submarine acquisition and support. Although MOD has taken into account its need for these skills, its significant future maritime programme likely will have to be modified or augmented to sustain these technical skills in the long term.

This is the key conclusion of a study of naval technical skills that RAND Europe pursued on MOD's behalf between 2006 and mid-2007. The study, the second investigation of demand for maritime labour in the UK that RAND has performed for MOD, is the first to investigate specific technical skills that the UK's maritime industry will need to sustain to preserve the country's ability to design, build, and support complex warships and submarines.

What Is the Problem?

The UK is pursuing several shipbuilding programmes—including the *Astute* submarine class, the Future Aircraft Carrier (CVF), the Future Surface Combatant (FSC), Military Afloat Reach and Sustainability (MARS) vessels, and the Type 45 destroyer—that may stress the UK's domestic shipbuilding and maritime support industry capacity over the next 15 years. Motivated by that possible overcapacity, MOD asked RAND in 2006 to help it better understand issues surrounding the UK's ability to sustain technical skills in its maritime sector.[1] In particular, it was interested in exploring the relationship between the demand created by its ship and submarine acquisition programme and the technical workforce needed to design, build, and support those war vessels.

MOD's future shipbuilding programme involves acquiring more than 50 ships and submarines over the next 30 years, according to official announcements and publications. To ensure that industry has the capability and capacity to fulfil this programme, MOD published its Defence Industrial Strategy (DIS) in December 2005.[2] This document established guidance for policymakers with respect to industrial goals and capacity that the UK will need to fulfil its military acquisition programmes over the next several decades.

The section of the DIS pertaining to maritime industrial issues is referred to as the Maritime Industrial Strategy (MIS). The MIS identifies six strategic capabilities that the UK will need to retain to preserve the domestic ability to design, build, and support complex warships and submarines onshore: maritime systems engineering, shipbuilding and integration, submarines and nuclear propulsion, maritime combat systems, maritime support, and maritime systems and technologies.

What Was RAND Asked to Do About the Problem?

Previous RAND studies for MOD have taken a macro look at the types and numbers of professional and nonprofessional skills that MOD will need to fulfil its shipbuilding programme. But in this case, the MIS raised a set of related questions at the micro level about key capabilities, prompting MOD to seek RAND's further assistance on this project.

---

[1] In addition to the 2005 study (Arena et al., 2005), this research drew from several other studies that RAND conducted for the MOD on maritime industrial strategy issues, including John F. Schank, Jessie Riposo, John Birkler, and James Chiesa, *The United Kingdom's Nuclear Submarine Industrial Base: Sustaining Design and Production Resources*, Santa Monica, Calif.: RAND Corporation, MG-326/1-MOD, 2005.

[2] UK Ministry of Defence (2005).

Specifically, MOD sought assistance identifying the following labour implications of its shipbuilding programme:[3]

- technical industrial skills needed to design, build, and support the vessels outlined in the programme
- how these skills are represented in the UK's maritime industry
- how these skills are used to meet the demands of the programme.

How Did RAND Study the Problem?

We pursued our research using a variety of qualitative and quantitative approaches. Our qualitative efforts involved reviewing relevant research done by RAND and others, interviewing key industry personnel to obtain information about their technical workforce, and conducting a qualitative survey of industry. Our quantitative efforts entailed creating and conducting a quantitative survey of industry to seek estimates of the technical workforces that would be required to meet the estimated demand of the future MOD maritime programme under a variety of conditions.

We reviewed work performed by RAND and others about maritime industrial issues, both in the UK and the United States. In a linked path, we interviewed experts from a cross-section of the UK maritime industrial base using a survey instrument that we designed. Our initial qualitative explorations produced a list of key maritime skills used by industry, most of which were of a technical nature.[4] We used that list, shown in Table S.1, as the basis for the rest of our project.

The survey was extensive and sought qualitative and quantitative data from each company about their workforces and their views of the industry.

---

[3] It was beyond the scope of this study to analyse the relationship between demand and supply of the technical skills.

[4] Throughout the rest of this monograph, we refer to this skill set as *technical skills*.

Table S.1
RAND Maritime Technical Skill Categories

Group	Skill Category
Detailed designers	Electrical and control
	Mechanical/fluids
	Hull/structural/arrangements
	Other detailed design
Professional engineers	Acoustics/signatures/dynamics
	Combat systems and integration
	Electrical and control
	Mechanical/fluids
	Naval architecture/marine
	Hull/structural/arrangements
	Testing, commissioning, and acceptance
	Safety/environmental
	Welding/metallurgy/materials
	Propulsion
	Nuclear specific
	Other engineering
Technical managers	Programme management
	Planning and production support

We used data that we obtained from the survey to populate a computer model, which we employed to project shipyard industry demand for labour under a variety of conditions in the future. The model that we used was a labour demand model that RAND has employed in many projects, but we modified it to incorporate technical skills identified in our qualitative survey.

During the course of the project, it became apparent that it would not be possible to incorporate the data from the support organisations and key suppliers that we surveyed. We omitted these data because they did not fully represent the support yards and suppliers across the maritime sector and could be misinterpreted. Although this meant that we had to exclude support, repair, and upgrade activities from the detailed demand analysis, presented in Appendix A, some analysis on how the limited data we collected may be added to the wider analysis.

What Did RAND Find Out?

What Did Industry Tell Us About Their Technical Workforce?

RAND sent the survey to key UK maritime industrial firms. The survey asked them to report how many detailed designers, professional engineers and technical managers they employ on UK maritime programmes. They reported that they employed a total of 3,525 personnel in technical fields within the maritime industrial base in 2007. Of these, 998 were employed as detailed designers, 1,842 were employed as professional engineers, and 685 were employed as technical managers.

The age distribution of this workforce was skewed toward older workers, with about half (46 percent) being older than 45 years of age. See Figure S.1 for more detail.

According to the survey, industry recruited this workforce in a variety of ways. Inexperienced technical labour tended to come predominantly from universities. Experienced technical workers came from a far greater variety of sources, including the aerospace, civil nuclear, and oil and gas industries. In addition, the maritime industry turned to former military professionals to fill certain experienced roles.

In the survey, the firms indicated that a number of specific technical skills were difficult to recruit: naval architects, electrical engineers (especially power engineers), systems engineers, and mechanical engineers. They qualified their answers, however, with the proviso that *experienced* holders of these skills were difficult to recruit, rather than that the skill was difficult to recruit per se.

The survey also asked how many years it would take technical skilled workers to achieve their optimum level of productivity. Although

Figure S.1
Age Profile of UK Maritime Technical Workforce

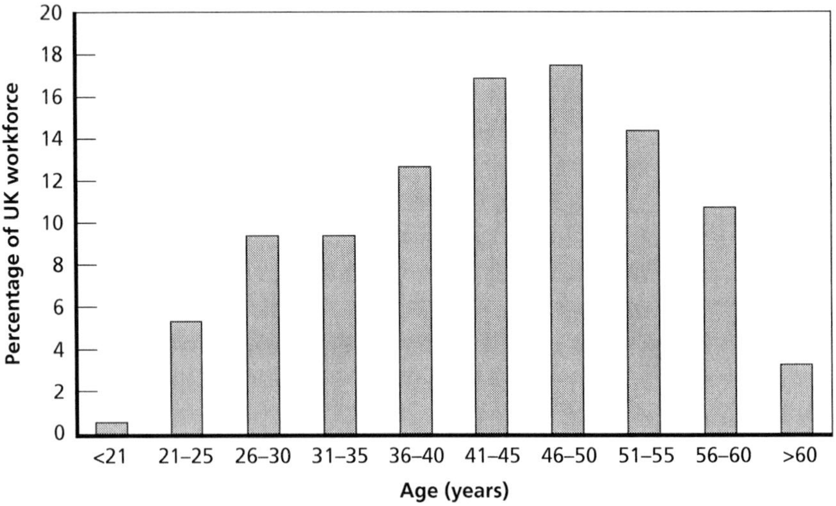

RAND *MG725-S.1*

the speed varied among different technical skills, firms reported that, on average, it takes six to eight years for all skills to reach 90 percent of the optimum level of productivity.

Finally, the survey revealed that industry anticipates a growing demand for IT design and electrical engineering skills in the coming decade.

What Is the Demand for Labour at the Aggregate Level?

We found that total labour demand for *all* skills required by MOD's future shipbuilding programme will rise steeply until 2013, reaching a level that will be two times the long-term average demand. Demand created by the complex surface ship programme is dominated by CVF in the near term, and decreases considerably in the longer term. The submarine programme places a more constant demand at the total labour level of analysis, though this demand varies over time. Total demand for all *technical* skills generally mirrors demand for all skills. However, technical skills are generally used in the earlier stages (the design and build processes) of maritime vessel programmes. Figure S.2 shows skill demand for detailed designers and professional engineers.

Figure S.2
Total Detailed Designer and Professional Engineer Demand, by Ship Class

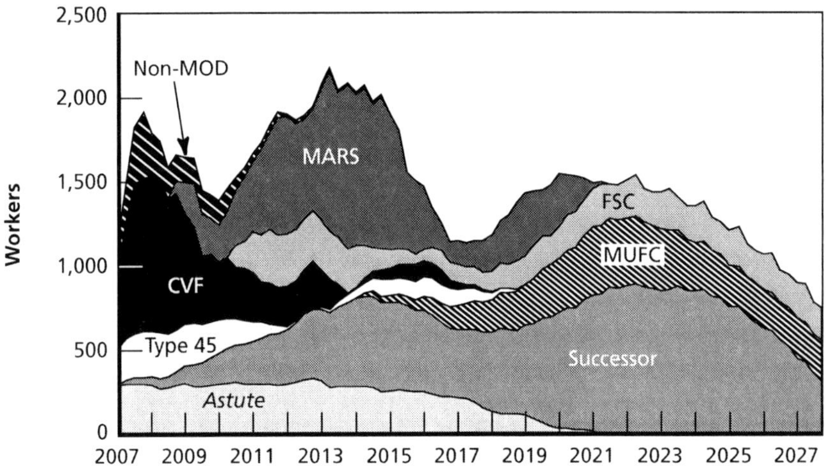

NOTE: MUFC = Maritime Underwater Future Capability.
RAND *MG725-S.2*

What Is the Demand for Labour at the Individual Technical Skill Level?

After looking at labour demand at the aggregate level, we looked at demand for the specific technical skills listed in Table S.1. In the context of complex surface ships, we found that sustaining detailed designer skills will be difficult after the design work connected with the first-of-class FSC is completed. Figure S.3 shows this potential skill gap.

We also found that MOD's complex warship programmes have a continuing, variable demand for professional engineer skills. An initial peak in demand from the CVF programme will be followed by a trough as that carrier programme winds down and as the final hulls for the Type 45 programme are completed. The FSC then provides a constant demand. Figure S.4 depicts this demand profile.

For the submarine sector, the CVF programme could be a vital bridge, providing demand both for submarine detailed designers and for professional engineering skills prior to the start of the Successor new design. Without demand from the CVF programme, there would

Figure S.3
Technical Labour Demand for Detailed Designer Electrical and Control Skills, Complex Surface Ship Programmes

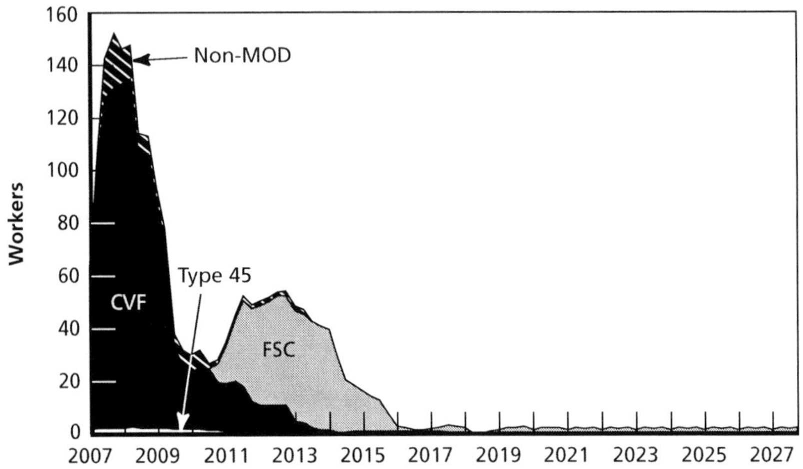

RAND *MG725-S.3*

Figure S.4
Technical Labour Demand for Professional Engineer Mechanical/Fluids Skills, Complex Surface Ship Programmes

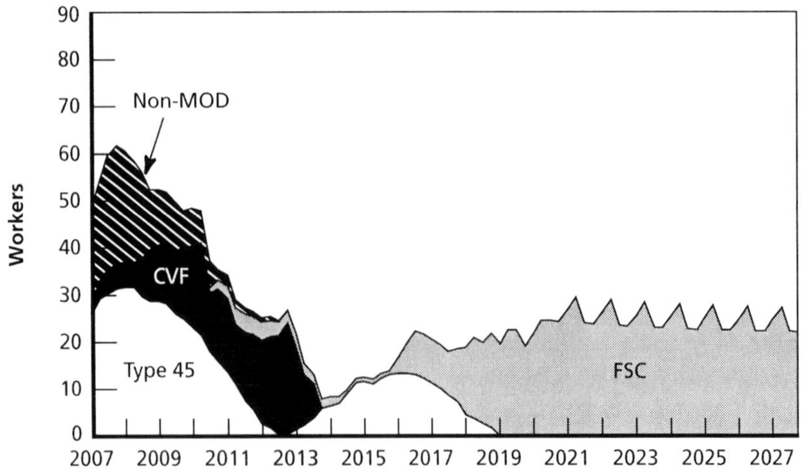

RAND *MG725-S.4*

be insufficient demand for most individual technical skills to sustain the capabilities that MOD desires to fulfil its requirements for a deterrent submarine design.

What Policy Conclusions Can the UK Ministry of Defence Draw from RAND's Findings?

Looking at this analysis more broadly, some general trends emerge with regard to future demand for design and engineering technical skills in both the submarine and surface ship sectors.

- *The MOD baseline programme will need some modification to help sustain the technical skills that support key industrial capabilities. The nature of the modification and its implementation require further investigation.* In the complex warship and submarine sectors, there are periods of low activity (such as a lack of work for detailed designers post–FSC design) which will not sustain those technical skills. Some technical skills may require programme additions or targeted initiatives if they are to be sustained.
- *Overall, there is sufficient demand from the submarine programmes to sustain design and build technical skills until 2027, although beyond this, the situation is less clear.* There are no gaps in technical labour demand from design/build submarine programmes for the next 15 years. The difficulty in this period will be to manage the increases in skills needed to deliver the Successor and MUFC programmes. The relationship between the end of these programmes and the start of any future submarine programmes will affect the demand that will sustain these skills. The CVF programme serves a valuable "bridging" function by providing additional workload to technical skills at the submarine shipyard. In the support sector, the demand on technical skills is much more variable.
- *The complex surface ship sector is more fragile than is the submarine base with regard to design/build skills.* Demand for detailed designer skills varies greatly in the near term and, following the FSC first-of-class design work around 2012–2016, there is little

future activity to sustain these skills until the start of a (postulated) Type 45 replacement programme. Should MOD decide to change the maritime surface programme and trigger, for example, reductions in new hull numbers, gaps in demand for professional engineer skills will develop quickly and may make them difficult to sustain. However, when one examines the support programme, the demand for technical skills in the complex surface ship sector is much more steady.

- *A specific maritime programme demand sustains detailed designer and professional engineer technical skills in different ways.* Detailed designers are in most demand during the design process of first-of-class ships or submarines. Professional engineers are involved more equally across the design and build processes, but demand varies for any given hull and between successive hulls. Both sets of skills work together during the design process, and demand for one invariably affects the other.
- *Examining MOD labour demand requirements at different levels of aggregation highlights different trends and challenges.* By looking at labour demand at a variety of levels (total labour, technical labour, detailed design/professional engineer, and individual skills), different trends are revealed. This ability is important, as it allows those making decisions about the future shipbuilding programme to better understand how they might affect the maritime industry.
- *There is a need to review technical labour demand requirements as programme assumptions change.* Any changes to MOD's ship or submarine programme assumptions will affect technical labour demand. Sometimes, changes that may be made to solve one problem may exacerbate another. The model that RAND has developed allows MOD to investigate and understand the industrial consequences of changes to the maritime programme and so aid longer-term planning; it should be used when programme assumptions change.
- *Recruiting certain technical skill sets will be challenging for industry.* Our industry interviews and survey highlighted the challenges of recruiting technical staff of the appropriate skill type and expe-

rience. Specifically, respondents highlighted difficulties finding and recruiting experienced professional engineers who are naval architects, electrical (power) engineers, systems engineers, and mechanical engineers.

- *As processes develop and technologies mature, the required mix of technical skills will change.* The technical skills needed today may not be required in the future. In our interviews and survey responses, industry anticipates increasing requirements for IT skills and electrical engineers. Working practices are also forecast to change, leading to, for example, greater remote working and a need for wider language skills. Again, MOD may wish to engage with industry to stay attuned to these trends so that its industrial strategy can sustain the skills that will be needed in the future.

Acknowledgments

This monograph would not have been possible without the assistance and support of many firms and individuals. First, we would like to thank our project sponsor, Jonathan Ackland of the Maritime Industrial Strategy team within Defence Equipment and Support, for providing invaluable guidance and intra-MOD coordination for the research team. Neil McCabe, Stephen Logan, and Mike Hollyhead of the MIS team also provided constructive direction for the project. Our thanks also go to DG Ships, Andrew Tyler, and the MIS Board for their support and sponsorship of this work. The authors would also like to acknowledge the shipbuilding Integrated Project Team leaders and members who participated in this study and provided insight and data about their programmes.

Within the wider shipbuilding industry, we are indebted to the shipbuilders, marine contractors, and suppliers who participated in the study survey and subsequent interviews. Without their assistance and cooperation, this research would not have been possible. Specifically, we would like to thank (alphabetically) Sean Donaldson and John Howie (Babcock), Bruce Durant (VT Shipbuilding), Richard Foran (DML), Paul Karas (Fleet Support Limited), Paul Moriarty and George Thompson (BAE Surface Fleet Solutions), Nik Moss (Thales UK), Roy Quilliam and Muir MacDonald (BMT Defence Services, Ltd.), Duncan Scott and Huw James (BAE Submarine Solutions), and Paul Wrobel (QinetiQ). Additionally, we thank the UK Naval Engineering, Science, and Technology forum for their contributions and suggestions.

We also thank our reviewers, Jessie Riposo and Arthur Fisher, for their thoughtful comments and suggestions, which greatly improved the final document. Within RAND, we would also like to acknowledge the assistance of Greg Hannah, Clifford Grammich, Kimberly Curry, and Neil Robinson, who assisted with background research and interview support, as well as Joan Myers and Debbie Peetz, who provided outstanding administrative support. John Birkler and the RAND MOD fellow, Paul Robinson, also supplied welcome wisdom and perspective to the project.

Although the individuals and organisations mentioned here helped us with data collection and analysis, we are are fully responsible for the interpretation of the information received and conclusions drawn, and, thus, we alone are responsible for any errors.

Abbreviations

CAD	computer-aided design
CVF	Future Aircraft Carrier
DIS	Defence Industrial Strategy
DSA	Design Support Alliance
EP07	UK Ministry of Defence 2007 equipment plan
FSC	Future Surface Combatant
HVAC	heating, ventilation, and air conditioning
IPT	integrated project team
JCTS	Joint Casualty Treatment Ship
MARS	Military Afloat Reach and Sustainability
MIS	Maritime Industrial Strategy
MOD	UK Ministry of Defence
MUFC	Maritime Underwater Future Capability
NSRP	nuclear steam raising plant
PR08	UK Ministry of Defence 2008 acquisition planning round
RFA	Royal Fleet Auxiliary

UK NEST	UK Naval Engineering, Science, and Technology (forum)

CHAPTER ONE

Introduction

The UK Ministry of Defence (MOD) is in the midst of a significant programme to renew and update its naval fleet. In addition to continuing its *Astute* submarine and Type 45 destroyer programmes, MOD anticipates placing other warship orders. As of this writing, these are the future aircraft carrier (known as CVF),[1] the Future Surface Combatant (FSC) frigate replacement, and the Successor nuclear deterrent replacement submarine. In addition, MOD expects to invite tenders for other classes of ships, including several new types of support ship.

This period of heightened activity is unusual, given trends in recent years and expectations of future ones. UK shipbuilding, both of commercial and military vessels, has been decreasing for years.[2] The number of surface combatants delivered each year to the Royal Navy has declined steadily, and demand on shipbuilding will diminish even further after the pending flurry of design and production. The intervals between production of new classes of vessels have also increased. Where, for example, there once was a gap of only eight years between first-of-class project acceptance dates of the *Valiant* and *Churchill* class and the *Swiftsure* class, in more recent times, there has been a 16-year gap between the *Vanguard* and *Astute* classes. All these trends raise

---

1 In July 2007, MOD made a commitment to place orders for two CVFs.

2 John Birkler, Denis Rushworth, James Chiesa, Hans Pung, Mark V. Arena, and John F. Schank, *Difference Between Military and Commercial Shipbuilding: Implications for the United Kingdom's Ministry of Defence*, Santa Monica, Calif.: RAND Corporation, MG-236-MOD, 2005.

several questions about retaining capability and supporting necessary skills in the maritime industry.

This research, sponsored by MOD, explores which maritime industrial skills could be considered critical to the key industrial capabilities described in the Maritime Industrial Strategy (MIS) and provides MOD with tools to investigate what might be done to maintain them.

Current Issues in UK Shipbuilding and the Maritime Industrial Strategy

The UK's decision to renew and upgrade its naval fleet will lead to varying demands on shipyard resources in coming years. These challenges are not unique to maritime procurement but reflect a trend that affects other parts of defence procurement. Overall, MOD has an ambitious procurement programme that has the potential to affect the future of industries in many sectors.

Defence Industrial Strategy

To address these industrial issues, in December 2005, MOD published its Defence Industrial Strategy (DIS), which was a follow-on to its Defence Industrial Policy of 2002.[3] We present extracts from the DIS here, together with relevant discussion, to aid understanding and refine the background of this project.

The aim of the DIS is to "promote a sustainable industrial base, that retains in the UK those industrial capabilities needed to ensure national security."[4] It describes which industrial capabilities are thought of as "sovereign" and so need to be kept within the UK (or "onshore") for every sector of industrial activity that contributes to defence. The

---

[3] UK Ministry of Defence (2005) and UK Ministry of Defence, *Defence Industrial Policy*, Ministry of Defence Policy Paper No. 5, October 2002, respectively.

[4] UK Ministry of Defence (2005, p. 6).

other capabilities are described as open to international competition (i.e., eligible for "offshore" delivery).

Maritime Industrial Strategy

The section that deals with the maritime sector is referred to as the Maritime Industrial Strategy (MIS). It defines the maritime sector as

> that element of the Industrial Base which designs, builds, supports and disposes of all naval platforms and systems. It encompasses ships, submarines, and their integral systems; including propulsion, services, combat systems and combat system elements. It draws extensively on other sectors, such as Guided Weapons, Aerospace and C4ISTAR (Command, Control, Communication and Computers, Intelligence, Surveillance, Target Acquisition and Reconnaissance). Maritime capability is delivered by the effective integration of platforms and systems, and their through-life support.[5]

The strategy specifies that "onshore capability is driven by two fundamental strategic requirements: the need to support military capability throughout its life; and the ability to mount operations from the UK base."[6] It identifies six strategic capabilities that need to be retained within the United Kingdom. They are described as either to be retained ("must be retained," "will retain," and "shall retain") or as a "high priority" to be retained. These strategic capabilities are as follows:

- *Maritime systems engineering resource:* ". . . the suite of capabilities required to design complex ships and submarines, from concept to point of build; and the complementary skills to manage the build, integration, assurance, test, acceptance, support and upgrade of maritime platforms through life."

---

[5] UK Ministry of Defence (2005, p. 68).

[6] UK Ministry of Defence (2005, p. 69).

- *Shipbuilding and integration:* ". . . a minimum ability to build and integrate complex ships in the UK. . . ."
- *Submarines:* ". . . capabilities unique to submarines and their Nuclear Steam Raising Plant (NSRP), to enable their design, development, build, support, operation and decommissioning."
- *Maritime Combat Systems:* "the ability to develop complex maritime combat systems is a high priority for the UK, and their integration into warships and submarines is an essential onshore capability."
- *Maritime support:* ". . . the ability to maintain and support the effectiveness of the Fleet, including incremental acquisition, generating force elements at readiness, and meeting urgent operational requirements."
- *Maritime systems and technologies:* ". . . research, development and integration of specific key maritime systems and technologies."[7]

In other words, the strategy requires the United Kingdom to retain the sovereign ability to design, build, and support complex warships and submarines. The MIS carries on to explain this in more detail.

- *Shipbuilding and physical integration:* The "high-value capabilities needed for . . . operational independence" are singled out for special consideration. The strategy describes the "need to build onshore to the extent that it sustains the ability to design and integrate complex warships," including the ability to "learn and adjust designs whilst the first of class is being built." It is the "high complexity, value added aspects of ship build and platform integration that must be maintained under UK sovereignty." Some aspects of the basic build process need protection, as it is "not effective to develop from scratch the most advanced, high-value skills needed for specialist hull construction or complex assembly tasks." Furthermore, there is a need for fabrication work to allow skill development of workers throughout their careers.[8]

---

7 UK Ministry of Defence (2005, p. 70).

8 UK Ministry of Defence (2005, pp. 70–71).

- *Submarines:* Nuclear ownership and commitments to the United States make it essential that the UK "retains the capability safely to deliver, operate and maintain these platforms, without significant reliance on unpredictable offshore expertise." The shipbuilding and integration requirements are reinforced by the specific "deep scientific and technical advice" and "specialist techniques, for example particular welding and fabrication processes," needed in the nuclear submarine industry.[9]
- *Maritime support:* This describes the related activities of operational support and refitting. The former demands a level of capacity and capability determined by the need to prepare warships, submarines, and auxiliary vessels for sometimes unexpected operations. Such support often involves the provision, installation, and integration of equipment that is highly classified. The strategy identifies as "key discriminators for provision of Operation Support" the "maintenance of national security and assured access to meet operational planning assumptions." Such activity would need to be undertaken onshore in almost all circumstances. The capability to refit complex warships onshore is needed because "[t]he infrastructure to conduct refits is extensive and not readily regenerated once lost" and it "becomes essential when security needs safeguarding . . . or control of the programme is strategically necessary" or during recovery from operations when "embarked ammunition is often involved." Further, "[t]he requirement to refit the submarine flotilla onshore is absolute."[10]

Key Industrial Capabilities Outlined in the Maritime Industrial Strategy

The key industrial capabilities that support the required and high-priority activities are identified against the relative onshore capacity requirement as shown in Figure 1.1, which we have reproduced from the DIS.

---

9 UK Ministry of Defence (2005, p. 71).

10 UK Ministry of Defence (2005, p. 72).

The dark portions of Figure 1.1 represent areas in which MOD wants to retain onshore capacity; these are described as the high-value activities and are focussed on definition, modelling and analysis, and design, on the one hand, and test and acceptance and support on the other. The light portions represent areas in which MOD believes that there is potential for offshore participation in future shipbuilding programmes, which are centred on the nontechnical capabilities, such as assembly and outfitting. Of note, the skill requirements surrounding the dark shaded areas tend to reside within higher-value technical skills, such as design and engineering, although certain production skills (particularly in the support domain) also fall within these areas.

Figure 1.1
MOD Estimate of Skills Required Onshore to Define, Design, Produce, and Support Military Vessels

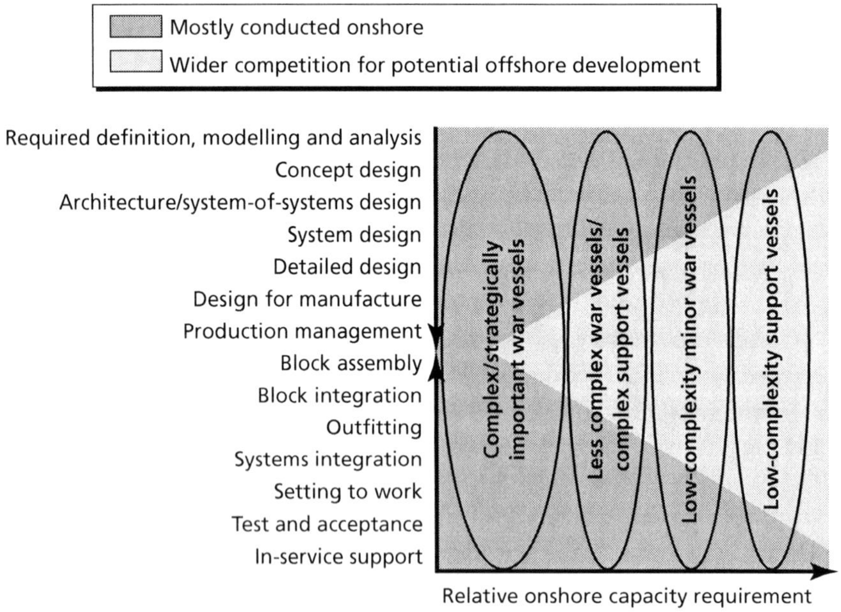

SOURCE: UK Ministry of Defence (2005, p. 69, Figure B2[ii]).
RAND *MG725-1.1*

Core Workload Outlined in the Maritime Industrial Strategy

The MIS recognises that MOD demand is needed to sustain the key capabilities. It states that "[t]here will be a minimum level of activity, or Core Work Load, necessary to sustain the key capabilities."[11] This minimum level of demand will not only sustain the identified key capabilities, but also provide value for money to MOD, be attractive to industry and be commercially viable. The strategy goes on to say,

> The Core Work Load will contain all the activity unique to submarines. For surface ships it is possible that only a proportion of the total programme in any given period may be required to sustain key capabilities. This core is likely to be centred on, though not necessarily restricted to, an onshore build capability for large complex warships.[12] This activity will provide the necessary experience for the management of build, integration and testing across the wider maritime programme. The Core Work Load will include support activities to prepare and deploy UK forces.[13]

The MIS addresses sustainability of the design capabilities by linking those for new build and in-service support: "By combining the new build and support design activities in a rationalised manner, a more sustainable capability is possible."[14]

In detail, and to summarise the MIS in terms that are relevant to this project, after the high level of demand from the CVF programme, the core workload requirements comprise

- the design and build of the alternating Destroyer and Frigate surface ship programmes (currently Type 45, then FSC, and then the Type 45 follow-on)[15]

---

[11] UK Ministry of Defence (2005, p. 75).

[12] The implication here is that "onshore build" will require onshore design. This is the intention described elsewhere in the strategy, as we have shown earlier in this chapter.

[13] UK Ministry of Defence (2005, p. 75).

[14] UK Ministry of Defence (2005, p. 76).

[15] There is no current MOD programme for a follow-on to the Type 45 destroyer. We postulate that there will be such a programme, similar to that of the Maritime Underwater Future

- the design and build of the alternating Attack and Deterrent submarine programmes (currently *Astute*; then the replacement for the *Vanguard* class, which is known as Successor; and then the *Astute*'s replacement, the MUFC)
- the support of these war vessels and others in the Royal Navy and Royal Fleet Auxiliary (RFA)
- additional activity, yet to be determined or agreed on, that will sustain the key industrial capabilities when the above demands do not.

Skills Needed to Accomplish the Maritime Industrial Strategy

For MOD to sustain its key industrial capabilities and define an appropriate core workload, it needs to understand the individual skill requirements which underpin these. Once MOD understands what skills are important, how they contribute to its future maritime programme, and how the future programme sustains these skills, it will be able to fulfill many of its requirements under the DIS. As mentioned earlier, many of the skills required by the MIS appear to be technical in nature, as the strategy places greater emphasis on the up-front design and engineering of complex warships and submarines, the testing and commissioning of new ships, and supporting these vessels through life. In discussions with MOD and industry representatives, we were told that these technical skills formed the basis of the key skills required to fulfil the requirements of the MIS; this is described in greater detail later. Thus, in this monograph, we look more broadly at technical skills in the maritime industry (particularly within the design/build and repair shipyards) to inform MOD about the interrelationships between these skills and the future MOD shipbuilding programme.[16]

Capability (MUFC), which continues submarine demand, otherwise the FSC programme will be the last MOD surface ship demand (which is unlikely).

[16] We explain later in this monograph that we excluded support/repair/upgrade activities from the demand analysis due to poor input data (both in terms of availability and quality). We present in Appendix A some analyses on how the support data we collected may be added to the wider analysis.

Organisation of This Monograph

The issues outlined in this chapter are addressed in separate chapters. Chapter Two is devoted to a description of the analytical and modelling methodologies that we employed. Chapter Three defines the technical skills that we addressed in this study and provides insight into their selection. Chapter Four reviews the qualitative and quantitative survey of industry that we conducted regarding the use of these key skills. Chapter Five examines different levels of aggregate demand for labour requirements generated by the current MOD warship programme, while Chapter Six examines the demand for individual technical skills generated by the complex surface warship and submarine components of the programme, respectively. Chapter Seven provides our conclusions, while Chapter Eight discusses possible future research in this area.

This monograph also includes several appendices. Appendix A explores an alternative strategy to incorporate support and repair/refit labour into our modelling calculations; this is important, as support activities are a key part of the MIS. Appendix B explores work done to identify and understand key technical skills which are so specific that they are difficult to model quantitatively. Appendix C describes the shipbuilding labour modelling tool that we used. Appendix D describes the demand for individual technical skills created by MOD's baseline shipbuilding programme. Finally, Appendix E reproduces the survey that we sent to contacts in the UK shipbuilding industry.

CHAPTER TWO

Project Methodology and Data Sources

The aim of this project is to provide MOD with the ability to understand better how the demand of its maritime programme affects the technical skills in the sovereign industrial base. To deliver this research in the time available, we set out to address the following issues:

- Identify and define the technical industrial skills that support the key industrial capabilities that meet the design, build, and support requirements outlined in the MIS.
- Understand how these skills are currently represented in the UK's maritime industry.
- Model how these skills are used to meet the demands of MOD's ship and submarine programmes.

Analytical Methodology

To do this, we pursued parallel qualitative and quantitative paths, depicted in Figure 2.1. Our qualitative efforts involved reviewing relevant research done by RAND and others, interviewing key industry personnel to obtain information about their technical workforce, and conducting a qualitative survey of industry. These efforts helped us to identify the key technical skills and understand their contributions to the MIS. Our quantitative efforts entailed creating and conducting a quantitative survey of industry to seek data on their estimates of the technical workforces that they would require in the future and using

Figure 2.1
RAND's Qualitative and Quantitative Analytical Process

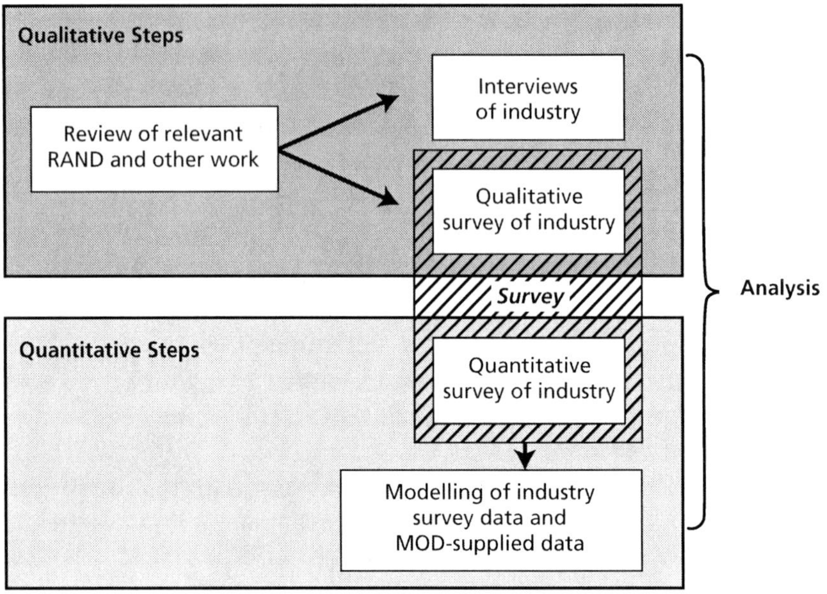

RAND *MG725-2.1*

these data to estimate demand for the future MOD shipbuilding programme under a variety of conditions. These efforts allowed us to numerically understand their importance to the future maritime programme. As shown in Figure 2.1, our survey effort spanned both qualitative and quantitative paths. We combined the results of these analytical efforts into our analysis.

We reviewed work performed by RAND and others on maritime industrial issues in the UK and the United States. In the first instance, the catalyst for this project was the earlier work *The United Kingdom's Naval Shipbuilding Industrial Base: The Next Fifteen Years.*[1] Our project specifically drew on this work, as we report elsewhere, as the baseline for approaching the challenge of identifying the technical skills in the UK's maritime industry. We drew on other RAND work, too, to aid our understanding of the UK industry, to refine a list of the

1 Arena et al. (2005).

potential technical skills needed to support the industrial capabilities, and to validate our new data as we received and analysed it. With regard to our modelling output, we wanted to either ensure continuity with any previously identified trends or isolate and explain any exceptions.

In a linked path, we interviewed experts from a cross-section of the UK maritime industrial base to aid in our understanding of the skills needed to support the key industrial capabilities described in the MIS. This is discussed in Chapter Three. We used these interviews to explain this project and to gain insight into the skills used to design, build, and support the maritime fleet. We also needed to gain interviewees' support and agreement to supply the large amount of data required for the quantitative portions of our research.

To gather data, we constructed a survey instrument, circulated it to potential recipients for comment, and then formally submitted the survey to them for completion. The survey, discussed in Chapter Four and reproduced in Appendix E, was extensive and required qualitative and quantitative data from each company about its workforce and its views of the industry. We qualitatively analysed these data, which we present elsewhere in this monograph, and used much of the survey's quantitative data in our modelling path.

Our labour demand model has been used in many projects and was particularly important for our first analysis of the UK shipbuilding industry. For this monograph, we needed to modify the model to allow us to incorporate the identified technical skills. We also made changes to tailor the user interface and outputs to MOD requirements. Appendix C describes the model in greater detail.

The output of the model is quantitative, and we show some of it in Chapters Five and Six. Here, too, we have provided a qualitative discussion of this output to show how MOD can now understand better the relationship between its ship and submarine programme demand and the technical workforce in the maritime industry.

Data Sources

Qualitative Data Sources

We relied on several sources for our qualitative evaluations. These included companies involved in warship design, production, and support: Babcock Engineering Services, BAE Systems Submarine Solutions, BAE Systems Surface Fleet Solutions, BMT Defence Services Ltd., Devonport Management Ltd., Fleet Support Limited, QinetiQ, Rolls-Royce, Thales UK, and VT Shipbuilding.

In addition, we interviewed key MOD personnel to gain insight into the future MOD shipbuilding programme.

Quantitative Data Sources

Our quantitative data came from a variety of sources. To populate our labour projection model, we relied on industry sources, including some of the companies listed above. We verified and supplemented these sources with existing RAND data.[2] We obtained production demand data from MOD as a result of an earlier, separate modelling activity. Design and production time frames were largely provided by MOD sources and all other collected data were verified with the appropriate platform integrated project teams (IPTs). Similarly, numbers of each ship class and acquisition strategies were also provided by MOD. Table 2.1 shows the sources of the data that we used in the labour projection model.

Table 2.1
Data Sources for Labour Projection Model

Type of Data	MOD	Industry	RAND
Specific skill profiles	X	X	X
Ship class numbers	X	X[a]	
Hull design/build time frame	X	X[a]	

[a] Export ships only.

---

2 There were also instances in which we had to modify profiles to fit MOD's schedules. This happened when industry assumed build periods that were slightly different from those of the MOD programme.

CHAPTER THREE

Identifying and Defining Key Skills

This chapter describes the key technical skills that we identified as appropriate to survey and model to answer the research questions. Here, we outline our research approach and look at relevant recent RAND work that has addressed maritime industrial skills and provided an initial platform to discuss these skills. We begin with a description of the industrial processes that bring a ship or submarine to life and maintain it: the design process, the build process, and the support process that keeps a vessel in service.[1] Then, we show our breakdown of the technical skills that industry uses in these processes. Finally, we relate the industry processes and the technical skills to the key industrial capabilities outlined in the MIS.

Approach and Initial Skill Definition

We used a series of iterative, qualitative steps to identify the appropriate technical skills for this project. We reviewed previous RAND work to provide a rough-order cut of potential skills which formed our initial list of key skills; these were largely technical in scope. We then interviewed experts from MOD and the UK maritime industry to gather fuller descriptions of ship and submarine technical activities and to learn how they identify their needed skills and manage their technical manpower. From these steps, we formulated a skills framework that

[1] We do not consider the disposal of maritime vessels.

we circulated to the UK maritime industry and MOD for comment. Based on their feedback, we refined our list of skills, adding to it where necessary.

On the whole, the skills described in earlier RAND studies were derived only from the design process for a vessel, particularly nuclear submarines. In this work, we considered the design of complex warships and the build and support processes for warships and submarines to see what additional skills might be required.

We found that we were able to use a single set of skill categories to describe the technical workforce involved in the design, build, and support of warships and submarines in the UK.[2]

This set of skill categories builds on previous RAND work, which allowed us to initially define skills among designers and engineers in the categories shown in Table 3.1.[3] This served as our starting point for further discussions with UK industry personnel as to the appropriateness of these skill definitions across the ship design/build/support life cycle, which we discuss later in this chapter.

Further, recent elements of previous RAND work gave us insight into the way that some U.S. shipbuilders categorise the skills that they use to design nuclear submarines and which highlight how the complexity and size of any attempt to model demand on design skills would increase quickly as greater detail is sought. Each of these individual categories is made up of a number of subcategories—each with a number of subskills. Figure 3.1 shows an example of this disaggregation from earlier RAND work.

---

[2] It is important to stress that such a list represents a compromise among differences in the workforces and practices, both historical and otherwise, of several maritime yards under different ownership. For these reasons, we do not make definitive statements about the ability to interchange technical skills among different yards, especially among those involved in build and design and those involved in support. For now, we treat each skill category as a single group across the maritime industry.

[3] To link with previous RAND work centred on the U.S. maritime industry we retain the terms *designers* (draughtsmen) and *engineers* (chartered engineers) in Table 3.1. Subsequently, as shown in Table 3.2, we use the terms *detailed designers* and *professional engineers* to make the distinction and avoid confusion.

Table 3.1
Initial Aggregated Skill Categories

Group	Skill Category
Designers	Electrical
	Mechanical
	Piping/ventilation
	Structural
	Other
Engineers	Electrical
	Mechanical
	Fluids
	Naval architecture and structural
	Combat system
	Acoustics
	Planning/production
	Testing
	Management
	Engineering support
	Other engineering

This hierarchy of skills in Figure 3.1 shows how a specific skill group (at the top of the pyramid—electrical analysis, in this case) is made up of a number of technical competencies, which, in turn, are defined by a discrete set of technical skills (at the bottom of the pyramid).

Refining the Technical Skill Sets

Drawing on the aggregated skill categories shown in Table 3.1, we conducted a number of interviews with industry experts to refine and modify our original list to ensure that our final list accurately reflected the key skills required by the MIS. Using these interviews, and reflecting the industry design, build, and support processes within a ship's life cycle, we constructed the technical skill categories shown in Table 3.2.[4] In it, we have aggregated technical skills and show examples of each. Detailed designers, also called draughtsmen, are predominantly involved in the design process, with some of those undertaking detailed design, providing support to the build process. Professional engineers are involved in the design and build processes, although some of these engineers might undertake work only in one or other, and indeed might work only in one phase of that process.[5] Nevertheless, we do not make that distinction in our survey or presentation of results. Technical managers, the final group, are specialists who might manage the technical staff, oversee the programme, and provide the link between design and production.

It is important to note that our discussions with MOD and industry personnel resulted in a refinement of our skill list. Most obvious is the addition of a new category, technical managers. However, we also added a number of additional skills that industry experts felt were key to the design, build, and support processes for the maritime programme consistent with the MIS. Specifically, we combined the original design categories of mechanical and piping/ventilation, refined a number of the professional engineering category names to make them more reflective of the UK industry,[6] and added additional categories where needed (acoustics/signals/dynamics, safety/environmental, and

---

[4] Table 3.2 shows three groups: detailed designers, professional engineers, and technical managers. Initially, technical managers were categorised within the professional engineer group in our industry survey. However, after further analysis and expert interviews, we determined that it was more accurate to designate a separate class of technical skill. We include technical managers in this table for clarity and consistency with the subsequent presentation of our data.

[5] In this study we did not investigate the degree of interchangeability amongst personnel in any one technical skill. Such interchangeability is available only to a certain degree. While some personnel can apply their skills to any phase, others are specialists and are tied to particular phases.

[6] Such as changing "testing" to "testing, commissioning, and acceptance."

propulsion). These changes ensured that our skill list was now reflective of those key skills required by industry to carry out its obligations under the MIS.

Figure 3.1
Categorisation of Nuclear Design Skills

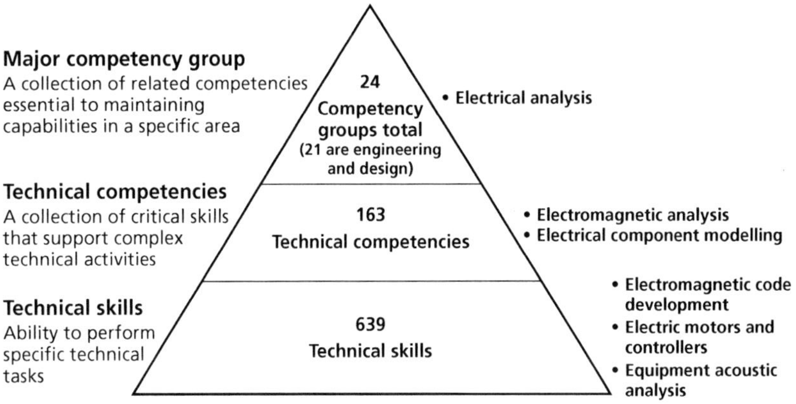

SOURCE: General Dynamics Electric Boat in John F. Schank, Mark V. Arena, Paul DeLuca, Jessie Riposo, Kimberly Curry, Todd Weeks, and James Chiesa, *Sustaining U.S. Nuclear Submarine Design Capabilities*, Santa Monica, Calif.: RAND Corporation, MG-608-NAVY, 2007.

RAND *MG725-3.1*

Table 3.2
RAND Maritime Technical Skill Categories

Skill Category		Examples of Detailed Skills
Detailed designers	Electrical and control	Electrical system component, electrical analysis, electrical design, power generation
	Mechanical/fluids	Mechanical component; mechanical system; mechanical design; piping design; heating, ventilation, and air conditioning design (HVAC); fluid system design; hydraulic system design
	Hull/structural/ arrangements	Structural engineering, structural arrangement, structural design
	Other detailed design	Engineering support, life-cycle support, software engineering, IT support

Table 3.2—Continued

Skill Category		Examples of Detailed Skills
Professional engineers	Acoustics/signatures/dynamics	Signature analysis
	Combat systems and integration	Combat system integration, combat system design
	Electrical and control	Electrical system component, electrical analysis, electrical design, power generation
	Mechanical/fluids	Mechanical component, mechanical system, mechanical design, piping design, HVAC design, fluid system design, hydraulic system design
	Naval architecture/marine	Naval architect, marine engineer, weights analysis, standards
	Hull/structural/arrangements	Structural engineering, structural arrangement, structural design
	Testing, commissioning, and acceptance	
	Safety/environmental	Safety engineers, environmental engineers
	Welding/metallurgy/materials	
	Propulsion	Shafting and gear design, prime mover analysis, propeller design and analysis
	Nuclear specific	Shielding, design, reactor plant design, turbine engineering
	Other engineering	Engineering support, life-cycle support, software engineering, IT support
Technical managers	Planning and production support	Scheduling, purchasing support, component support
	Programme management	Programme management, schedule and cost control, estimating

Ship or Submarine Life Cycle

The technical skills listed in Table 3.2 are in demand across a ship's or submarine's life cycle. For the purposes of this study, we defined *life cycle* as the processes through which the first of class of a new class of ship or submarine passes: design, build (or construction or production), and support.[7] Successive ships or submarines in the class that are unchanged will benefit from lessons learned from the first of class, will likely have reduced design and build processes, and so will place less demand on the detailed designer and professional engineer technical skills.

Design Process

The design process consists of four phases: concept design, preliminary design, contract design, and detailed design.[8]

- *Concept design:* In this phase, concepts are explored against a backdrop of a continuing evaluation of future missions, future threats, and future technologies.
- *Preliminary design:* During this phase, the preferred concept is matured. Subsystem configurations and alternatives are examined and analysed for their military effectiveness, affordability, and ease of production.
- *Contract design:* This phase consists of the transformation of the top-level requirements into contracts for the detailed design and construction of the vessel.
- *Detailed design:* This phase is normally performed by the shipbuilder, since it transforms the contract drawings and ship specifications into the documents necessary to construct, outfit, and test the vessel.

---

7 See, for example, Thomas Lamb, ed., *Ship Design and Construction*, 2 vols., Jersey City, N.J.: Society of Naval Architects and Marine Engineers, 2003.

8 These phases and descriptions are taken from Schank, Riposo, et al. (2005). Lamb (2003) uses *functional design* instead of *detailed design* and suggests that *contract design* and *functional design* could be called the *system design phase*. UK Defence Procurement Agency, *Warship Engineering Management Guide*, draft C, MAP 01-020, August 2005, describes the design process in more detail: option identification, design survey, design development and assessment, system design, contract design, and production design. In this monograph, in part for simplicity, we stick to the RAND structure and acknowledge that others are in use.

Build Process

The build process consists of planning, construction, and acceptance.[9] Recent advances in computer-aided design (CAD) and reviews of traditional procedures have led to integrated design and build processes.[10] As with the design process, we describe the traditional approach here.

- *Planning:* This phase is conducted by the shipbuilder and will overlap with all the latter design phases to provide necessary information to them.
- *Construction:* Construction involves the greatest number of non-technical workers, although they are increasingly expected to be multiskilled. Designers monitor construction to ensure that the vessel is built according to the plan, or where it is not, and deviations are reassessed for incorporation in the design or concessions are agreed to.
- *Acceptance:* Shipbuilders have their own quality-assurance systems that are built around the use of test forms, initial inspections, and final inspections.[11]

Support Process

The support process maintains the ship in service. The maintenance may be routine or occasional, major or minor, and any combination of these. Vessels may suffer accidents at sea that require unplanned, major rectification, for example, or routine minor maintenance may be planned for whenever the vessel is in port. Planned major maintenance periods will draw on the technical skills involved in the design and build of a vessel, particularly when MOD requires the introduction of new systems or extensive structural changes. Even in these circumstances, though, the technical skills will be exercised to a different

---

[9] Again, there are variations in describing this process, with, for example, acceptance separated from production.

[10] For example, see Schank, Arena, et al. (2007), for a description of how the *Virginia*-class design and build process has evolved from the traditional approach.

[11] We include this phase within the build process to capture the role of the shipyard in inspecting, testing, and commissioning all aspects of the ship.

extent and in different ways. For example, designing changes to an existing structure, where the detail is already established, is different from producing that detail on a blank screen or piece of paper.

Use of Technical Skills Across Vessel Life Cycles

Demand for detailed designers, professional engineers, and technical managers occurs throughout the design, build, and support processes. As depicted in the notional graphic display in Figure 3.2, the involvement of these designers, engineers, and managers varies over the design

Figure 3.2
Design and Build Demand for Technical Skills, Notional First-of-Class Complex War Vessel

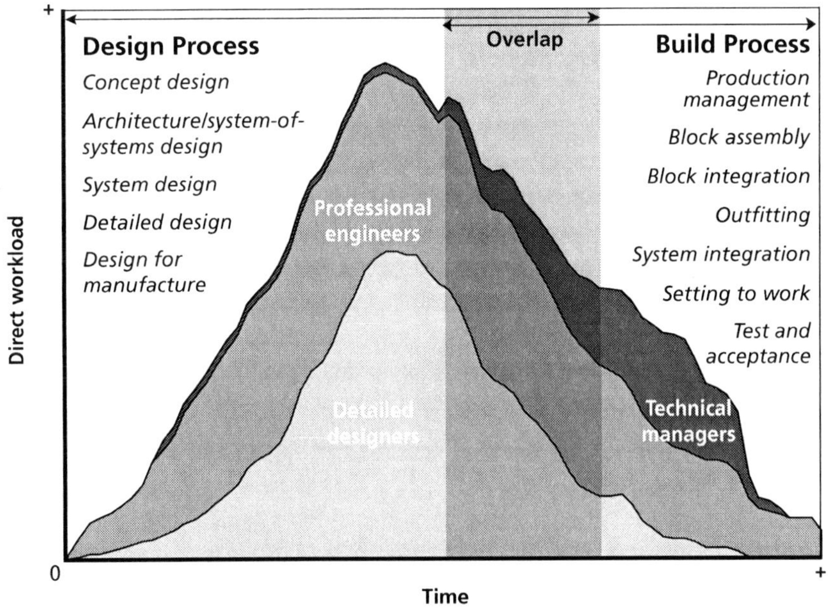

NOTE: Italics = MIS key industrial capabilities.
RAND *MG725-3.2*

and build life cycle of a vessel.[12] The leftmost portion of a figure represents the start of work by the shipyard on the design of a vessel, perhaps very early concept design or assisting MOD in refining the requirements. The limited technical management activity at this stage provides oversight of the programme and planning for later work. Design effort peaks toward the centre of the curve at about the same time that construction starts. At that point, the detailed designer effort focusses on the detailed design phase and support to the early phases of build, continuing to refine the detailed design as construction continues. Professional engineers continue to support the design effort and provide support to the planning and construction phases. Technical managers support production and are the link between the "paper" design and the employment of the production workforce. As the vessel nears completion, moving toward the right in the figure, design work completes and the involvement of detailed designers and technical managers diminishes. Professional engineers continue to provide support to construction and are now involved in the acceptance phase. The vessel is delivered at the point shown in the rightmost part of the figure.

We have superimposed a dividing area between the design process and the build process. Additionally, we have placed in the appropriate section MOD's key industrial capabilities, which we reproduced in Figure 1.1 in Chapter One; we have associated these capabilities with the relevant design and build processes. Cumulatively, this figure shows the technical skill profiles and their nominal relationships to the industrial design and build processes and the key industrial capabilities of the MIS.

---

12 We show here a simplified and modified output from our model of a first-of-class complex war vessel.

CHAPTER FOUR

How Technical Skills Are Represented in the UK Maritime Industry

This chapter presents the results of an extensive survey designed by RAND and sent to key UK maritime industrial firms for completion. The goal of the survey was to gather data from each firm on its current workforce profile, to gain insights into the firms' experience in the demand for and availability of specific technical skills, and to collect information on the performance characteristics of these skills once in employment.

This chapter begins by detailing the research methodology employed in devising the survey. This is followed by a discussion of the survey data and presentation of the most salient observations from the industry responses. The chapter concludes with a summary of the main observations arising from the survey responses.

Research Methodology

We based the design of our industry survey on the technical skills that were identified in Chapter Three.[1] Additionally, we wanted to gain a

[1] As described in Chapter Three, the study team identified a number of skill categories to represent the major technical activities undertaken by the UK naval shipbuilding industry. The resulting top-level technical skill list, as based on a number of subskills, formed the basis upon which many of the quantitative survey questions were designed. The qualitative survey questions sought to tease out more general observations surrounding the issues of assembling and maintaining a technically skilled workforce.

more qualitative understanding of the human-resource issues involved in developing and maintaining a skilled technical workforce. We then consulted firms in the UK maritime industry to ensure that the survey was appropriately attuned to their conception of maritime labour and sent them a preliminary list of questions for initial comment. We also conducted preliminary visits to firms to discuss the selection of technical skills and to clarify ambiguities surrounding the kinds of data and the level of detail required. Following these discussions, we modified the survey as appropriate.

Consequently, the survey asked a mix of quantitative and qualitative questions about each firm's technical skills and workforce and requested future workload demand estimates by technical skill category. A copy of the survey is included in Appendix E.

Who We Asked

We sent the survey to seven UK firms that primarily work in ship design, production, and support:

- Babcock Engineering Services
- Babcock Naval Systems[2]
- BAE Systems Submarine Solutions
- BAE Systems Surface Fleet Solutions
- Devonport Management Ltd.
- VT Shipbuilding
- Fleet Support Limited.

We also sent the survey to four key UK maritime suppliers:

- BMT Defence Services Ltd.
- QinetiQ
- Rolls-Royce
- Thales UK.

---

[2] Babcock Naval Systems did not provide a complete survey response but did review the findings of our work.

We recognise that these four firms perform critical roles in the supply of specific maritime systems, but they do not represent an exhaustive list of all key UK maritime suppliers. We have therefore treated their responses as indicative, but not representative, of the key supplier sector of the UK maritime industry. Their qualitative comments appear in the subsequent analysis for this purpose.

Survey Results

The following sections present the key findings from the survey answers that we received. This analysis is based on the quantitative data and the qualitative comments of key industry respondents.[3]

Current Technical Skill Breakdown

Our survey asked industry to report how many detailed designers and professional engineers they employ on UK naval programmes. Table 4.1 shows the total size of those workforce segments employed in design/build and support yards.[4]

---

[3] Where possible, we have aggregated the data we received in the survey responses into the primary categories of tasks that each firm performs. We have termed these ship design or build and ship support. The former category includes maritime yards that are primarily involved in the design and build of submarines and surface ships. The latter category includes maritime yards that are primarily involved in overall support activities. While we recognise that the tasks performed by each respondent are not entirely limited to one of the sectors of activity described, and that a degree of design, production, and support activities may all take place at a single site, we have chosen to cluster responses for two reasons. First, it affords us the opportunity to present the survey data in a meaningful way by profiling the industrial workforce through a task-driven categorisation. Second, by clustering the survey data, we will subsume the identity of individual respondents and respect their desire to protect commercially sensitive information.

[4] The data shown in this section and used subsequently in the modelling do not include figures from the key suppliers that we surveyed; we omitted the key supplier data because it did not fully represent the suppliers across the maritime sector and could be misinterpreted. These supplier firms have other technical skills (e.g., scientists, system designers) that also contribute to the UK maritime programme. The data also do not include many of the detailed designers who are subcontracted from other firms to assist the maritime industry in their detailed design work.

Table 4.1
Number of Detailed Designers and Professional Engineers Employed in UK Complex Design/Build and Support Yards, 2007

Skill Category		Design/ Build Total	Support Total	Grand Total
Detailed designers	Electrical and control	96	114	210
	Mechanical/fluids	140	126	266
	Hull/structural/arrangements	189	129	318
	Other detailed design	32	172	204
	Subtotal	**457**	**541**	**998**
Professional engineers	Acoustics/signatures/dynamics	25	7	32
	Combat systems and integration	235	28	263
	Electrical and control	60	39	99
	Mechanical/fluids	89	85	174
	Naval architecture/marine	59	31	90
	Hull/structural/arrangements	47	47	94
	Testing, commissioning, and acceptance	258	141	399
	Safety/environmental	33	41	74
	Welding/metallurgy/materials	19	7	26
	Propulsion	5	26	31
	Nuclear specific (e.g., shielding)	53	204	257
	Other engineering	159	144	303
	Subtotal	**1,042**	**800**	**1,842**
Technical managers	Planning and production support	331	23	354
	Programme management	226	105	331
	Subtotal	**557**	**128**	**685**
Total, by respondent		**2,056**	**1,469**	**3,525**

Table 4.1 shows that 3,525 personnel worked in technical fields within the maritime industrial base in 2007. Detailed design technical skills tend to be based within submarine yards and support yards, while the professional engineer base is more evenly spread across the industry. The testing, commissioning, and acceptance skill set has the largest number of personnel, employing 399 individuals. The firms surveyed employed fewer than 50 individuals in a number of skills (welding/metallurgy/materials, acoustics/signatures/dynamics, and propulsion). A number of other skills have fewer than 100 personnel across the industry (safety/environmental, hull/structural/arrangements, naval architecture/marine, and electrical and control).

Technical Skill Age Profiles

We also surveyed the age spread of the UK maritime workforce. Figure 4.1 shows the overall age profile of the technical skills included in the survey. The figure illustrates that the overall technical workforce skews toward older workers, with about half (46 percent) being older than 45 years of age. This is more or less true within the age profiles for specific technical skills, although some stand out as having age profiles that are particularly skewed toward older ages. These include the engineering skills of combat systems and integration (64 percent over 45 years old); acoustics/signature/dynamics (58 percent over 45); testing, commissioning, and acceptance (56 percent over 45); and programme management (52 percent over 45).

Conversely, some technical skills stand out as having age profiles particularly skewed toward younger ages. These include the engineering skills of naval architecture/marine engineers (75 percent under 45), hull/structural/arrangements (67 percent under 45), mechanical engineers (64 percent under 45), and electrical and control designers (62 percent under 45).[5]

We break down this age demographic further into detailed designers and professional engineers, as depicted in Figures 4.2 and 4.3.

---

5 A possible reason for this younger age distribution, as indicated in our conversations with industry, is that many younger engineers will first train in their general skill prior to moving onto a more specialised area.

Figure 4.1
Age Profile for UK Naval Technical Workforce

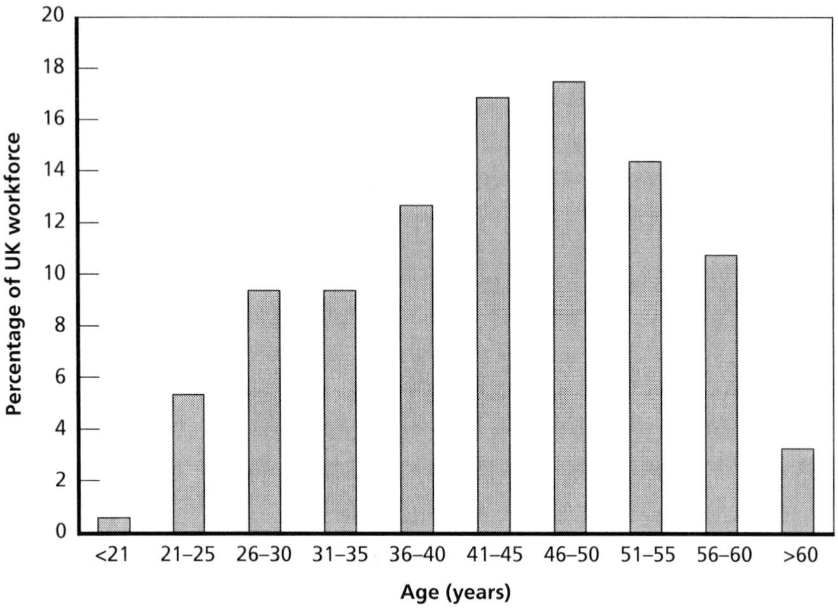

RAND *MG725-4.1*

Figures 4.2 and 4.3 show that the age profile of professional engineers slightly diverges from that of detailed designers, with the former having an older distribution than the latter. A greater percentage of professional engineers (47 percent) were over 45 than was the case with detailed designers (40 percent). The largest single demographic group for professional engineers was 46–50 years, while for detailed designers, the largest cohort was younger (41–45 years). However, the clear majority of workers were over 35 years of age—75 percent in both cases.

Recent Hiring/Leaving Trends

In addition, we asked industry to identify the technical skills that had dominated their hiring over the past five years, as well as those skills that represented the greatest number of *voluntary* departures during the same period. Table 4.2 shows, in rank order, the results.

Figure 4.2
Age Profile for Professional Engineers

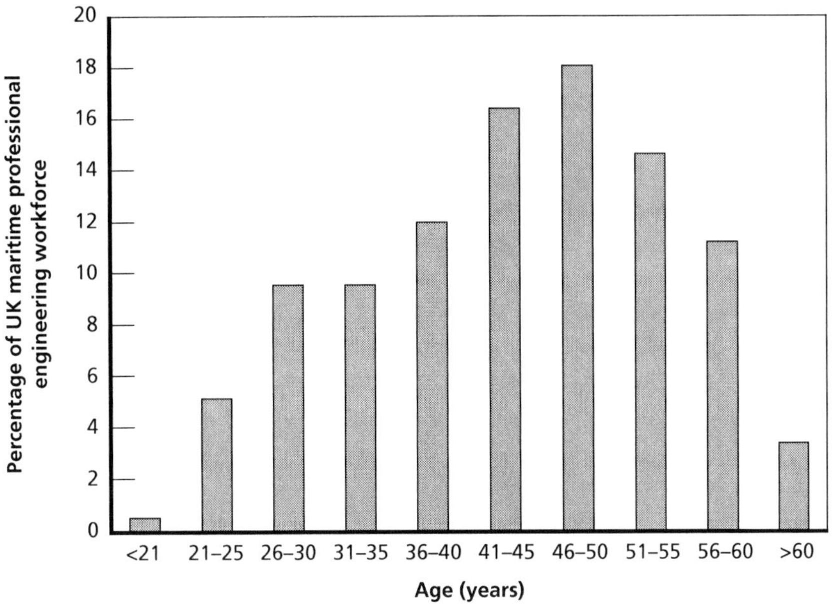

NOTE: Because our survey included technical managers within this grouping, the age profile data presented here also include those skills.
RAND *MG725-4.2*

The first observation is that the top five in rank order in both categories are professional engineering and technical management skills. The data show that naval architects/marine engineers; programme managers; and testing, commissioning, and acceptance engineers tended to have higher turnover than do those with other maritime technical skills: All three ranked highly in both hiring and voluntary departures. The emergence of the requirement for nuclear-specific skills is likely linked to the design and build requirements for the *Astute*-class submarines.

Technical Skill Sourcing and Availability

The sources from which UK maritime firms seek to recruit technical skills vary according to whether the firms need experienced or inexperienced labour. One industry respondent commented that their balance

Figure 4.3
Age Profile for Detailed Designers

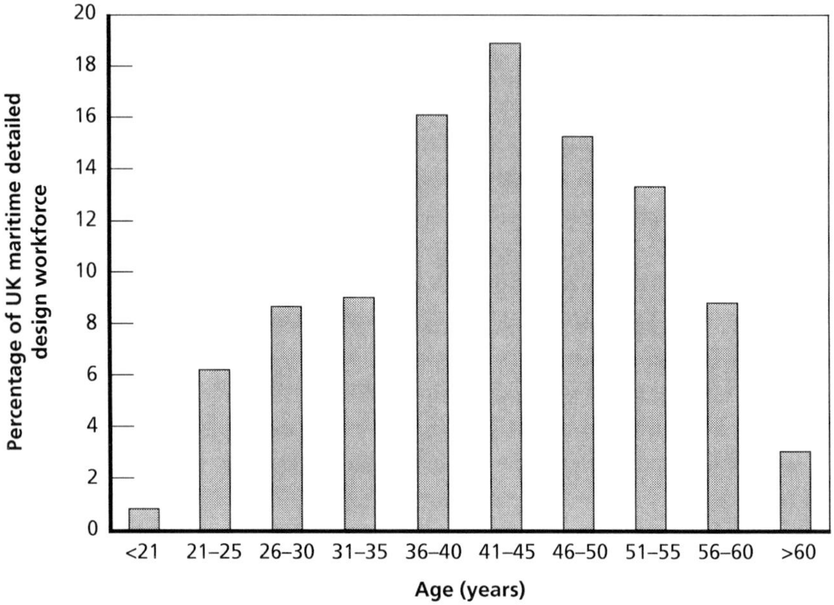

RAND *MG725-4.3*

Table 4.2
Top Five Maritime Technical Skills by Hiring and Voluntary Departure, 2002–2006

Top 5 Skills Hired	Top 5 Voluntary Departures
Nuclear specific (e.g., shielding)	Programme management
Hull/structural/arrangements (engineer)	Naval architecture/marine
Naval architecture/marine	Planning and production support
Testing, commissioning, and acceptance	Testing, commissioning, and acceptance
Programme management	Mechanical/fluids (engineer)

of recruitment was 40 percent inexperienced and 60 percent experienced workers, although this will vary by firm.

Regarding sources of recruitment for hiring workers new to the industry, there was unanimity from the different industry respondents. All focus on university graduates, and some do so through dedicated graduate-recruitment schemes that are operated in partnership with certain universities. Some universities are targeted for their subject-specific reputations in science, engineering or the maritime industry. Included in the list of institutions mentioned were Birmingham, Glasgow/Strathclyde, Imperial College London, Newcastle, Portsmouth, Southampton, and University College London. Others, such as the University of Bath, were specified for their locality. An industry respondent estimated that 85 percent of inexperienced hires entered the firm through a graduate training scheme. The remaining 15 percent were said to be recruited as apprentices from schools and colleges, subsequently receiving specialist trade training from their employer.

To recruit experienced technical workers, firms turn to former MOD, Royal Navy, and other armed forces personnel, especially for roles that relate to combat systems and other warship-specific areas. However, recruiting experienced labour from within the naval and broader maritime industry was highlighted as an option made increasingly difficult by the finite number of individuals in this field. Several respondents talked about the "poaching" of skilled labour that occurs among the major UK yards. Some of the larger firms reported that they have tried to overcome this by boosting internal recruitment and by looking to other areas of the wider company that may house comparable skills.

Given shortages within the industry, the most common recruitment source cited for experienced labour was from industries outside the maritime sector that foster comparable or applicable skills. The sheer variety of industries that were cited by respondents made it clear that this has come to encompass an increasingly wide variety of relevant industries. Examples of the most commonly cited industries included aerospace, automotive, blue-chip companies (for managerial roles), construction, heavy mining, large engineering companies, nuclear, oil and gas, and petrochemicals. Some respondents described limiting their search to industries in which the basic skill set can be readily adapted to the maritime defence market, although the variety of industries cited indicate that this is interpreted increasingly broadly. Other respondents specified that the recruitment source was very much dependent upon the particular skill set that was being sourced. Consequently, the use of headhunters or specialist recruitment agencies has become an increasingly common mechanism for facilitating this recruitment of experienced skilled labour.

To place the recruitment sources of experienced labour into context, one key industry respondent provided the following details: 40 percent of the firm's workers were from hired from competitors within the defence sector; 40 percent were hired from comparable industries outside the sector, and 20 percent were former MOD or Royal Navy professionals.

When asked to identify any existing untapped sources for potential recruitment, the respondents unanimously highlighted foreign labour, particularly given the difficulties in meeting recruitment requirements from exclusively UK sources. The use of European sources was stated, with some success in recruiting from Eastern Europe, including Romanian and Polish nationals, but also further afield, including labour from India. The viability of these sources is tempered by security concerns surrounding foreign labour working on MOD naval technology, particularly nuclear technology.

A variety of specific skills were highlighted as being particularly difficult to recruit, although there was less commonality because respondents were focussed on their particular area of the industry. For example, yards that produce or support submarines tended to highlight nuclear-specific skills. A large number of skills were cited once in the survey responses as being difficult to recruit, and four technical skills were highlighted by several respondents as being troublesome to recruit:

- naval architects
- electrical engineers (especially power engineers)
- systems engineers
- mechanical engineers.

Often, answers were qualified with the specification that experienced holders of these skills were difficult to recruit, rather than the skill being difficult to recruit per se. Most respondents tied their answers regarding recruiting difficulties to competition with other industries for skilled labour. This included competition with many of the industries listed earlier that are themselves being tapped for the maritime sector's recruitment needs.

Productivity Curve by Technical Skill

We also surveyed the number of years that it takes a newly hired worker to become proficient enough to reach his or her optimum level of productivity.[6] This is important to understand because simply employing a worker in a specific technical skill does not intrinsically equate to possessing the associated workforce capability—experience is critical in ensuring that the technical skill becomes a productive capability.

We have chosen to illustrate these data as a "productivity curve," which traces the rate at which each technical skill discipline increases in productivity (see Figure 4.4). A steep curve indicates that optimum productivity is reached comparatively quickly after commencing employment. A more gradual curve indicates that greater time in employment is required before optimum productivity is reached.

We have chosen to group all technical skills into a single cluster (the shaded area in the figure) to illustrate the broad pattern of increasing productivity.

Figure 4.4 illustrates that, based on an average taken from the respondents' answers, it would take 6–8 years to reach at least 90 percent of optimum productivity. A number of skills deviate from this general trend. In particular, acoustics/signatures/dynamics and nuclear-specific skills stand out as those that were noticeably slower to reach optimum productivity—these skills constituted the lower side of the shaded area. Safety/environmental and welding/metallurgy/materials engineers exhibited something of a lag, but this was slight in

---

[6] Survey respondents had individual definitions of the optimum level of productivity. We understand that this introduces a level of subjectivity but feel that the results are useful to convey.

Figure 4.4
Productivity Curve by Technical Skill, Build and Support

RAND *MG725-4.4*

comparison. Conversely, programme management exhibited far greater speed to reach optimum productivity and is represented in the upper side of the shaded area. The remaining skills are tightly clustered in the shaded area.

We also looked at data specific to the ship build and ship support survey responses. Within the ship build data, safety/environmental engineers and hull/structural/arrangements designers displayed the greatest time lag before achieving optimum productivity. Conversely, programme managers and testing, commission, and acceptance were the fastest to achieve optimum productivity.[7]

Different trends within ship support back up these data. The technical skills that took the greatest time to achieve optimum productivity were nuclear specific and acoustics/signatures/dynamics. Noticeably,

---

[7] Based on our conversations with industry personnel, this is possibly attributable to new hires in these technical skills already possessing experience prior to employment.

the three detailed designer skills (electrical and control, hull/structural/arrangements, and mechanical/fluids) were the quickest in reaching optimum productivity.

Mentoring New Hires

The survey inquired about the number of inexperienced people who could be mentored by an experienced worker. This was asked to determine how industry uses its experienced workforce to train and develop its less experienced workforce.

Regarding on-the-job training for engineers, a ratio of one to one was commonly stated as the ideal. Some respondents stated that, to avoid compromising their own ability to work, a professional engineer can develop only a single inexperienced person at a time. If this ratio is increased to include more inexperienced people, the productivity of the mentor is likely to drop. Respondents commented that if charged with more than two trainees, the engineer ceases to be a worker able to manage key deliverables and outputs and starts becoming a dedicated trainer. However, respondents commented that as trainees become more independent, the ratio can increase to cover two or three inexperienced people without compromising the effectiveness of the trainer to such an extent.

Regarding the mentoring of professional roles (such as management activities), a ratio of one experienced person to three inexperienced persons were described as effective. It ought to be stressed that there was no overall consensus on the ideal ratio. Individual industry respondents have their own conceptions of this, with some responses stating that up to 12 staff members could be mentored. One respondent commented that, typically, 20 percent of staff in a department may be "inexperienced."

Skill Demand Driven by Specific Programmes

The survey asked whether certain technical skills were unique to specific programmes and not utilised in other types of activities, and whether this varied by type or class of vessel. A number of responses stressed skills that are specific to submarine programmes. A respondent provided the opinion that, although submarine designers can be used to work on surface ships, surface ship designers find it more difficult to work on submarines.[8] Those familiar with the sector posited the following skills as requiring specialised application for working on submarines:

- mechanical and electrical systems (due to safety, shock requirements, and redundancy)
- nuclear design, build, radiation, and shielding (due to parameters and specifications very different from those of the civil engineering environment)
- weights, welding, and materials (due to differing requirements for surface vessels)
- acoustics/signatures (a specific and major requirement for submarines)
- combat systems (ability to integrate submarine specific sensors, weapons, and combat management systems)
- test and commissioning (familiarity needed with the performance requirements, safety, and trial programmes specific to submarines)
- project management and planning (though generic sector knowledge is also vital).

Key suppliers working in the submarine sector commented that while they prefer to foster multiskilled engineers who possess transferable skills, certain, specific skills are required. These include expertise in hydrodynamics, manoeuvring and control, structures, propulsion, acoustics, and atmosphere control. Another respondent commented that certain submarine-specific capabilities are not easy to diversify into other business areas. Some of these submarine- and nuclear-related skills were also marked by several respondents for their specificity—that is, the difficulty for technical workers outside of the submarine/nuclear domain to work on these programmes.

---

[8] This statement was made by an individual working outside of the submarine domain.

Future Trends in Demand for Skills

The survey closed by asking industry respondents for their opinions on the coming decade, how they foresee future technical activity differing from what has gone before, and whether any skills sets will become redundant during this period while others emerge as more needed. Demand for the following skills was seen as becoming more prevalent in the future:

- *IT systems and associated skills:* A greater degree of integration between the design process and the production process might drive changes in skill demands. A number of survey respondents cited greater emphasis on IT systems and associated skills. The impact would be felt primarily through the greater use of design software and its utilisation for modelling the design process, for storing technical information relevant for trials and tests, and for through-life support.
- *Management and organisation:* The potential need to adapt current management and organisation processes for effective design of through-life platforms was highlighted. This is driven by the need to step away from the current warship design process that tends to take each line of development independently and then bring them together at the build phase. The need to integrate expertise in staffing, life cycles, upgrading of systems, and other such support tasks into the design phase will require adapting current management practices.
- *Electrical systems:* There is some consensus around a likely future emphasis on electrical rather than mechanical systems. One respondent pointed to the changing need for electric propulsion in warships and submarines as bringing its own demand for skills at the potential expense of traditional skills, such as gearbox engineering. In a similar vein, electrical actuation and control may overtake demand for some hydraulic systems. The potential for electric propulsion and electric launch systems in the new aircraft carrier was presented by another respondent as creating greater demand for these skills. Also, combat and mission systems are

likely to become ever more complex, and a commensurate change in available skills will need to match these changes in technologies and systems.
- *Language skills/remote working:* Although not a technical skill, if tapping into foreign labour sources becomes an everyday reality for the industry, the potential future need for language skills would increase. Linked to this would be technology that will allow for remote working, if segments of work are to be completed offshore for later integration.

There was little consensus on skills for which demand might recede over the coming decade. The support sector pointed out that it is likely to be working on many of the vessels that are currently in service for much of this period. As proficiency with IT in design increases, some respondents foresee consequences, such as reducing the amount of time taken to get a new design into production and, perhaps, a reduction in requirements for traditional design skills involved in detail design stages (creation of manufacturing drawings, CAD inputs and outputs). Regarding engineering, automation might erode the need for the current amount of human activity in some technical production outputs (for example, steel cutting and burning, pipe manufacture, or more general production).

Observations

Based on the quantitative data and qualitative information collected through our survey, a number of observations can be formulated:

- *The current workforce profile is skewed to 45 and older.* Overall, about half of the technical workforce is over 45 years of age, and some specialist skill sets are older; however, many of the basic technical skill demographics are much younger and will specialise over time.
- *There is difficulty in recruiting experienced skilled technical labour.* All respondents spoke of widening the recruitment net to target

a diverse selection of unrelated industries from which to recruit experienced labour, and that competition is reciprocated by industries.

- *Many skills require considerable time before they reach optimum productivity.* The majority of technical skills take a number of years before workers are sufficiently experienced to reach levels close to optimum productivity. This "ramping-up" period varies according to sector and skill, with certain permutations taking considerably longer than others.
- *A number of skills require unique application in the submarine sector.* The greatest incidence of skill demands being driven by specific programmes is in the submarine sector. In part, this is due to the demands of the underwater environment and the technical challenges that submerged operation of a vessel poses. It is also because they are the only nuclear vessels (both in terms of propulsion and weapon systems), which brings additional challenges.
- *Some technical skills are difficult to recruit in the industry.* These include general skills, such as naval architects and systems and mechanical engineers, as well as more specialised skills, such as electric power engineers and nuclear-specific skills.
- *There is an anticipated growing need for IT design and electrical engineering skills in the coming decade.* The respondents made these speculations based on the current trend lines of increasing integration of design and production skills through IT and a shifting emphasis on electrical rather than mechanical systems.

CHAPTER FIVE

Total Labour Demand by Current MOD Maritime Shipbuilding Programmes

In this chapter, we provide results of our quantitative analysis of total demand for labour generated by all warships and submarines in MOD's maritime procurement programme. We described the sources of our data in Chapter Four. The data and assumptions that underpin our analysis model are described in more detail in Appendix C. As discussed previously, the RAND shipbuilding model has been used successfully to investigate demand and supply in the UK and U.S. maritime industries. Analysis at the highest level of aggregation, total labour demand, provides useful information about the general state of demand and how it might impact the supplying industry. Such techniques and the resulting analysis were used to inform the MIS. Although the focus of this research project is on key technical skills, we, by necessity, collected the data that allow output at the total demand level. We are thus able to update our previous work with a revised MOD programme and refined data from the shipyards.

Assumptions

Programmes Included in Our Modelling Activity

We used a specific definition of the MOD programme to identify the ships for input into the model. These programme assumptions were provided by MOD and reflect current thinking according to MOD's 2007 equipment plan (known as EP07), which is being further developed for application in the first phase of MOD's 2008 acquisition planning round (PR08).

- *Type 45 destroyer:* We assumed that future Type 45 destroyers would be built in the same modular way with no significant capability upgrades in the final batch of ships. However, some additional design work to take out cost was included in our projections, in line with current activities on ships in production.
- *CVF:* We assumed that the CVF would be built in four modular blocks of varying size, which would then be transported to a single location for final outfitting. We did not assume any non-UK involvement in the production of the vessels.[1]
- *Military Afloat Reach and Sustainability (MARS):* This programme is currently planned to encompass multiple ships of three types: fleet tanker, fleet solid support, and joint sea-based logistics. Our assumptions regarding the exact number and size of each type was informed by the most current thinking within the IPT. We assumed that a single MARS hull would be built in one location but that multiple locations could produce hulls, leaving open the possibility that the hulls could be produced offshore.
- *FSC:* Although we understand that there are multiple potential variants of the FSC frigate, we modelled only a single monohull structure that we assumed would be constructed at a single location.
- Astute *class*: We assumed that all follow-on *Astute* attack submarines would be built in a similar manner to the current hulls. However, we did assume some design upgrade activity for each successive hull.
- *Successor:* As the UK's next-generation deterrent submarine, we assumed that the Successor hull would have a new design but would be of a comparable size to the current *Vanguard* class and would be constructed using similar production methods as the *Astute* class.
- *MUFC:* We assumed that the follow-on attack submarine class to the *Astute* would have a new design but would be similar in size to the current *Astute* class and constructed using similar methods.

---

[1] Due to ongoing commercial negotiation, CVF programme workload assumptions were very dynamic, and our estimates are based on data from March 2007.

Programmes Not Included in Our Modelling Analyses

There were some MOD programmes which we did not include in our modelling activity, although the capacity exists to add these programmes to the model at a later date once better information is known. These include the following.

- *Landing-platform helicopter replacement:* Although it is reasonable to assume that HMS *Ocean* will go out of service within the time frame of this study, a replacement is not currently funded, and we have chosen to exclude it from the baseline programme.
- *Future mine countermeasure vehicles:* Again, we know that many of the current vessels will be scheduled for replacement within the study time horizon, but there was no consensus regarding type, number, or size of replacement ships.
- *Non-MARS RFA ships:* The only RFA ships included in the baseline programme in the model were the MARS family of ships. Our MOD sponsors did not see the utility of including any additional RFA-type ships in the baseline programme.
- *Assault ship replacements:* The two landing platform dock ships, *Albion* and *Bulwark*, have recently entered the fleet, and neither we nor our sponsors saw the need for us to include a replacement in the model.
- *Type 45 replacement:* Although the Type 45 destroyer will need to be replaced eventually, we felt that the timing for its replacement was beyond the time frame of our study, and any inclusion of a speculative programme would not be useful in our analysis. Of course, such a programme is likely, and, in keeping with the requirements of the MIS, MOD will need to understand how demand for FSC and this replacement affects demand on technical skills.

In addition to this basic information of which activities to include, we had to make assumptions around the length and specific timings of design/build activities for each hull and the utilisation of each of our skill categories over time. We also had to assume an acquisition strategy for each class of ship, including such points as the general characteristics of each ship and how it would be built (modular or single-site, for example). Through discussions with industry, MOD, and other stakeholders, we were able to construct a reasonable, but not definitive, projection of the future MOD maritime programme.

Additional Assumptions and Information

Unfortunately, comprehensive data at the specific skill level we required were not available to allow us to model refit/repair/upgrade information (either in terms of volume or time scales of work) to the granularity we desired. The support-yard personnel with whom we spoke in the support yards did not tend to capture their future requirements for technical work through demand projections; rather, they tended to operate on historical precedent and recruit specific skills as the need arose. Thus, we have not included this sector in our analysis. However, it is important to keep in mind that ship and submarine support activities may play a role in sustaining some key maritime skills. In an attempt to better understand the impact of these activities, we present further analysis in Appendix A.

Another area that we have not explicitly included in our modelling activity is those skills that are provided for by key equipment and lower-tier suppliers. Again, we acknowledge that these portions of industry also provide skills which MOD may look to sustain in the future; however, they were outside of the scope of the study, and we later recommend that MOD endeavour to study in the future the sustainment of the skills provided by key suppliers.

One additional set of data that we included in our modelling activity is that provided by known export orders which the UK maritime industry has won through competitive tender. Because we have included only known export orders won, the model is likely to understate the impact of these activities in the mid- to long term.

Skill Categories

Overall, we attempted to analyse the data using 15 skill categories. These largely aligned with the technical skill categories presented in Chapter Three. However, due to a lack of available data, we were not able to quantitatively model the technical skills associated with acoustics/signals/dynamics, safety/environmental, propulsion, and welding/metallurgy/materials. Additionally, we added a new labour category of production to account for blue-collar structural and outfitting workers and a variety of management and support activities which fall outside of our definition of technical skills. This allowed us to capture all of the labour present in maritime design, build, and support activities—although our analysis will be focussed on the technical skills. Thus the labour skill level categories that we examined were

- detailed designer
  - electrical and control
  - hull/structural/arrangements
  - mechanical/fluids
  - other (design skills that do not fit into the above)
- professional engineer
  - combat systems and integration
  - electrical and control
  - mechanical/fluids
  - naval architecture/marine engineer
  - hull/structural/arrangements
  - testing, commissioning, and acceptance
  - nuclear specific
  - other (engineering skills that do not fit into the above)
- technical manager
  - planning and production support
  - programme management
- production (blue-collar structural and outfitting skills, management and support skills not included in the technical skills above).

It is also important to note that the labour estimation model projects only direct labour and does not account for overheads that will be unique to individual shipyards, prime contractors, and design firms.

For our purposes, we define direct labour as labour specifically charged to a particular project.

Total Labour Demand

We examine first the highest level of output: the total direct workforce demand. At this level, MOD would be able to understand the overall shape of its labour demand, which, in turn, can serve as a rough proxy to measure financial costs of the future maritime programme. Figure 5.1 shows the total direct workforce demand on the baseline MOD programme.

In the figure, we show the cumulative effect of each of MOD's future programmes.[2] The area enclosed by any one programme reflects

Figure 5.1
Total Direct Workforce Demand, All Programmes

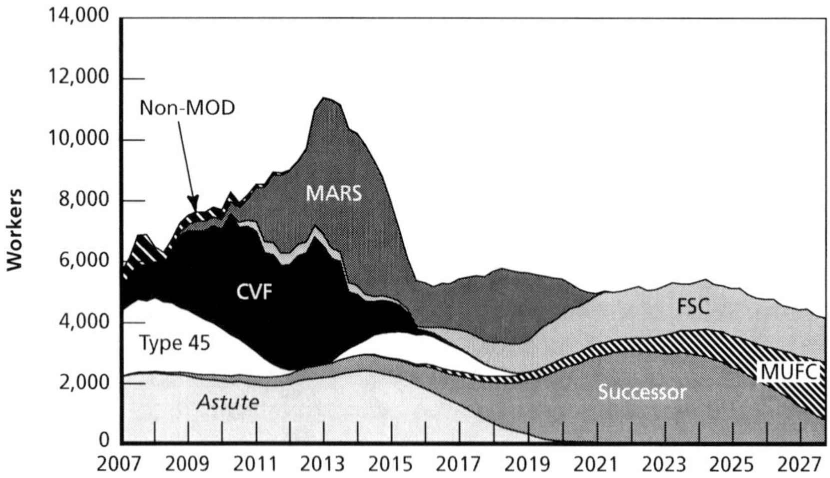

RAND *MG725-5.1*

2 Remember that we have excluded support/repair/upgrade activities from the demand analysis due to poor input data (both in terms of availability and quality). However, Appendix A provides some analysis on how the limited support data we collected may be added to the wider analysis.

its size, though at this level of detail it is not possible to see whether the total demand is biased toward technical workforce demand or non-technical demand. Many large but simple ships may have an overall demand similar to few, complex vessels. Such a case exists, for example, when comparing the MARS and Successor programmes. The figure shows that there is a gradual increase in overall demand, which peaks in the 2013–2014 period before returning to a longer-term steady demand broadly similar to the 2007 demand levels. Much of this increase appears to be due to the emergence of two programmes—CVF and MARS, particularly when their demands build on one other during the peak period.

Labour Demand: Complex Surface Ships

Such a picture of overall workforce demand gives a wider perspective of the challenges facing MOD and the maritime industry, but it is not representative of the policy outlined by MOD in the MIS. Further levels of detail are needed for this. Our next step is to consider the complex surface ship and the submarine programmes individually. We separate these programmes in this way for two reasons. First, this is how the UK maritime industry is structured. Secondly, the MIS articulates support for surface ships and submarines separately, too. A further reason, which may be of equal importance but that we are able to relate only qualitatively, is that for a variety of reasons, the workforces involved in surface ship and submarine programmes may not be easily interchangeable and so should be investigated only within those programmes.[3]

We look first at complex surface ship demand in Figure 5.2. Recall that MOD defines this element of the core workload as the

---

[3] We use *interchangeable* here to make the point that, as currently configured and due to geographic constraints, the workforces of the different surface ship and submarine yards do not tend to flow freely and generally remain associated with those yards (at this level of analysis). We are not implying that the workforce of any individual shipyard can only undertake work normally associated with that yard; for example, the submarine workforce at Barrow has designed and built surface ships. However, we heard a strong contention from our interviewees that the skills used in submarine design/build are more specific than those required for complex surface ships and that it is more difficult, but not impossible, to move from the latter to the former.

Figure 5.2
Direct Workforce Demand, Complex Surface Ships

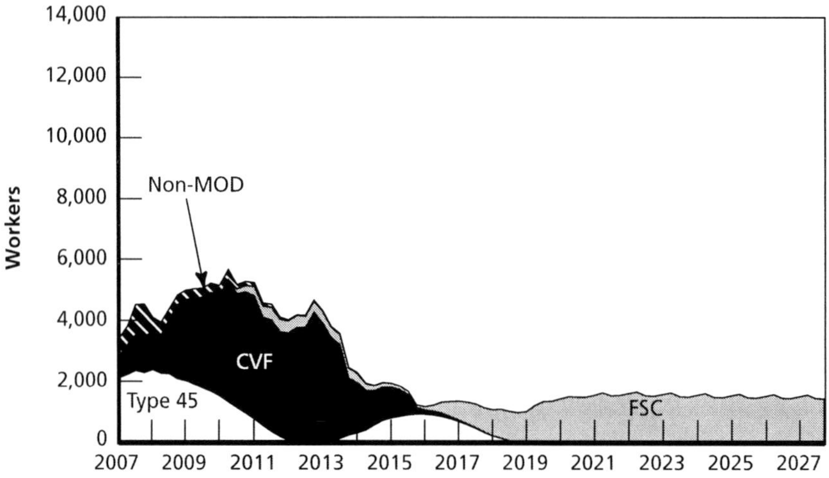

RAND *MG725-5.2*

Type 45 and FSC programmes. CVF is an additional programme that will place an exceptional demand on the UK maritime industry. Finally, in this figure, we show the export work reported by shipyards as a confirmed commitment. In this analysis, MARS is not part of the complex surface ship demand.

The impact of the CVF programme is easily seen in this figure.[4] Because of it, workforce requirements peak at just over 5,500 direct workers before substantially reducing to a steady state of around 1,500. It is also important to note that the Type 45 programme is split; the first six hulls are completed prior to a break, while CVF is at its height, before restarting to complete the final two hulls. The FSC programme represents the future steady-state demand for complex surface ships.

Labour Demand: Submarines

The workforce demand from the submarine programme is different, as can be seen in Figure 5.3. The work associated with the ongoing

---

[4] This is the total CVF demand. MOD and industry intend to split this demand across surface shipyards and those whose normal focus is submarine or support activity.

Figure 5.3
Direct Workforce Demand, Submarines

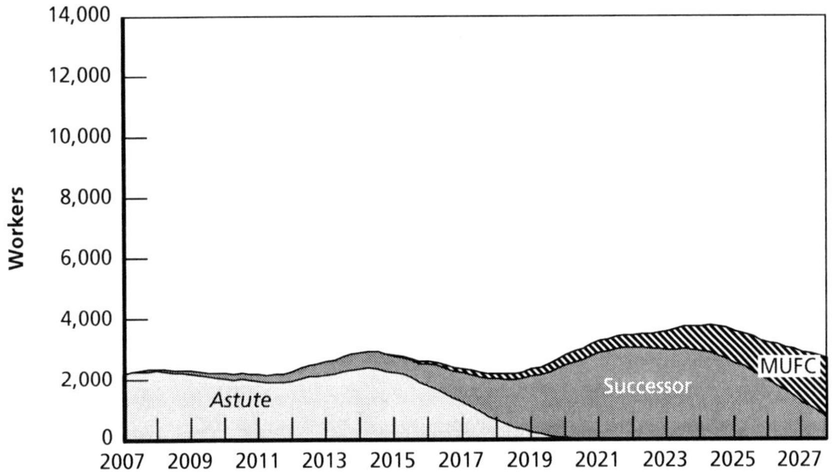

RAND *MG725-5.3*

Astute programme, followed by that for the recently announced Successor programme and the intended MUFC programme, combine to produce a steady demand of between 2,000 and 3,000 direct workers until 2020, when there is a gradual increase to about 4,000 workers as Successor and MUFC demands combine.

Examining these programmes in further detail, we can see *Astute* production tailing off between 2016 and 2020, as the seventh boat is delivered; Successor design starting in the near future prior to ramping up to production, within 10–15 years; and MUFC design activities beginning around 2014 with full production, again starting around 10–15 years after that. There is a slight complication for the submarine demand picture, however, caused by the need to split CVF work. The submarine programme is supported by one shipyard, and it is intended to undertake elements of the CVF programme; the effect of this is shown in Figure 5.4.

This figure shows demand on the UK's submarine shipyard from MOD's programmes. The impact of the allocated CVF work is marginal at this level of analysis, with two peaks of activity pushing

Figure 5.4
Direct Workforce Demand, Submarines and CVF Elements

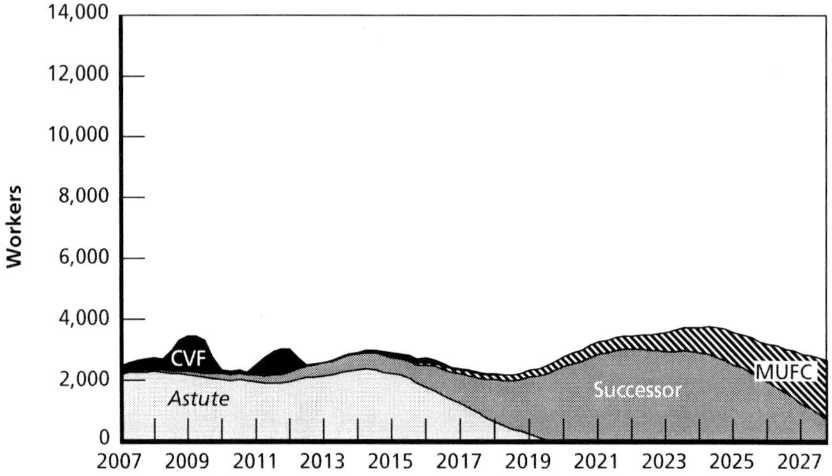

NOTE: In our analysis, we attempted to apportion workload among the different organisations responsible for design/build of CVF.
RAND *MG725-5.4*

demand to around 3,500 workers in 2009 and 2012. CVF adds slightly to the peak of demand from the underlying submarine programmes, around 2015.

Demand for Technical Skills

In the previous section, we used the model to show data at the highest level of labour demand. In this section, we consider demand at the technical skill level of detail, albeit with those skills combined.[5] We are not yet breaking them down by individual skill; this we will do in the next chapter when we consider the demands of the complex surface ship programme and the submarine programme separately. In this sec-

[5] The figures in this chapter include all of the subskills associated with the detailed designer and professional engineer skills defined in Chapter Three; they do not include technical manager skills.

tion, we repeat our look at the overall complex surface ship and submarine programme demands, restricting the data accordingly.

Figure 5.5 shows the total technical workforce demand, by ship class for the baseline MOD maritime programme. The vertical axis range of this figure differs from that of prior figures and runs to 2,500 workers. The figure shows that technical workforce demands generally mirror the wider workforce demands seen in Figure 5.1, but the programme peaks occur slightly earlier in time, reflecting the bias of greater technical workforce involvement in the earlier phases of the design and build processes. It is possible to place this profile into perspective by comparing the demand with the technical workforce supply data shown in Table 4.1 in Chapter Four. Our respondents' total workforce across surface ship, submarine, and support yards was 3,525 workers; across surface ship and submarine yards, the total was 2,056 workers.[6]

Figure 5.5
Technical Workforce Demand, by Ship Class

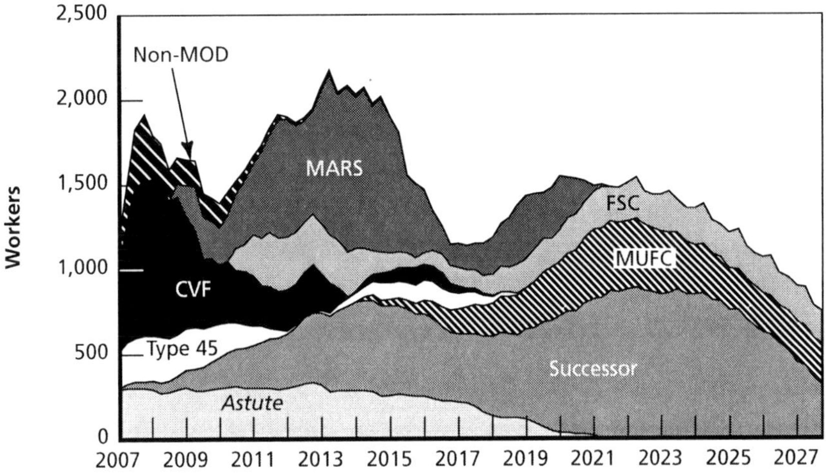

RAND *MG725-5.5*

[6] Note that some aspects of demand may be met by others involved in the UK's maritime industry. We show this comparison to give a better perspective of the level of demand. This

Demand for Technical Skills: Complex Surface Ships

The technical workforce demands on complex surface ships and submarines also differ from the corresponding overall demand profiles. Figure 5.6 shows the technical workforce demand of the complex surface ship programme. Whereas in the total demand profile, though showing significantly increasing demand, also shows that the CVF programme covered to some extent a trough formed by the completion of the sixth Type 45 hull and the delivery of the remaining two hulls of the class. The impact of the FSC programme at the total level of demand in this period was minimal. At the technical level, however, Type 45 and FSC provide level demand, in part because the early stages of FSC are dominated by the design process, and also because there is limited design support required for the final two Type 45 hulls. CVF and non-MOD work add to this demand. After the potential excessive demand of the CVF

Figure 5.6
Technical Workforce Demand, Complex Surface Ships

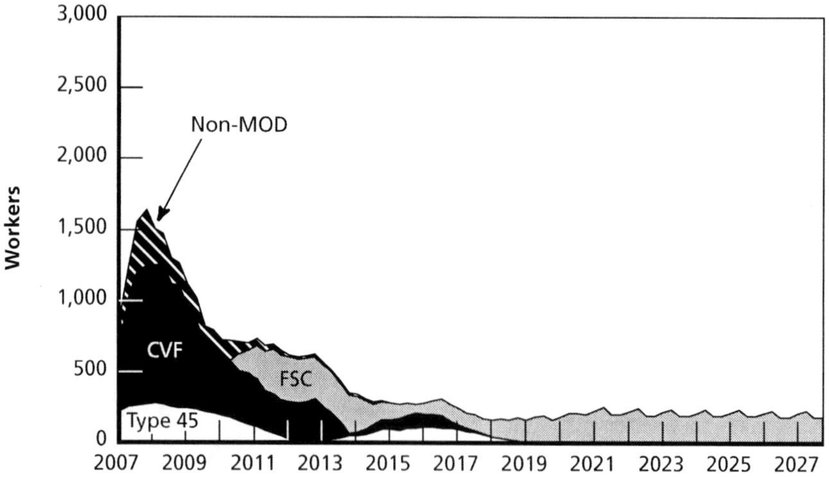

RAND *MG725-5.6*

---

will be more apparent as we explore technical skills in greater detail. Also, some of the technical skill numbers captured in the survey may be indirect (and not captured by our modelling activity).

programme, which will not fall completely into this grouping, and non-MOD work, the demand in this grouping will fall to about 300 workers. MARS is not shown in this figure, as it is not a complex surface ship.

Demand for Technical Skills: Submarines

Next, we examine the technical workforce demand of the submarine programme. We see in Figure 5.7 that demand on technical skills is different from that for the whole workforce, seen in Figure 5.3. Whereas that demand was relatively stable, the technical requirements ramp up significantly to account for new design activities: first for Successor and then for the MUFC programme. The technical workforce demand then increases further as multiple Successor boats enter production and the design activities of MUFC continue. We saw earlier, however, that some of the demand for CVF will be met by this workforce, and we show this in Figure 5.8. Here, we see the total technical workforce demand on the shipyard that focusses on delivery of MOD's submarine programme. The CVF element provides

Figure 5.7
Technical Workforce Demand, by Submarine Class

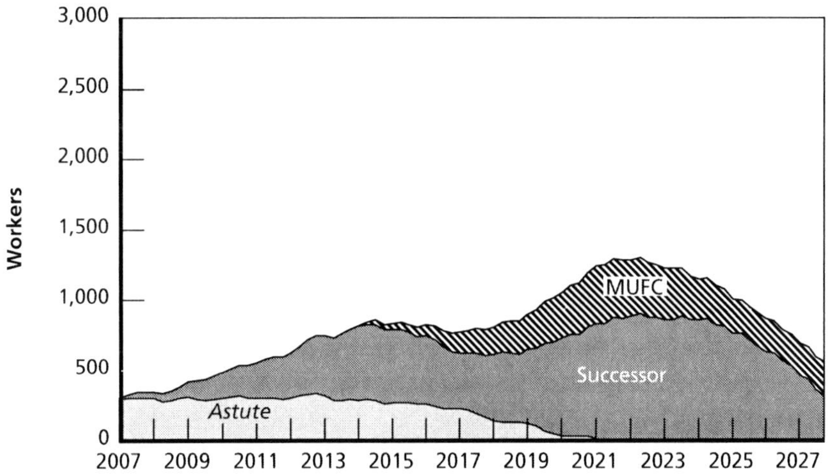

RAND *MG725-5.7*

Figure 5.8
Technical Workforce Demand, by Submarine Class and CVF Element

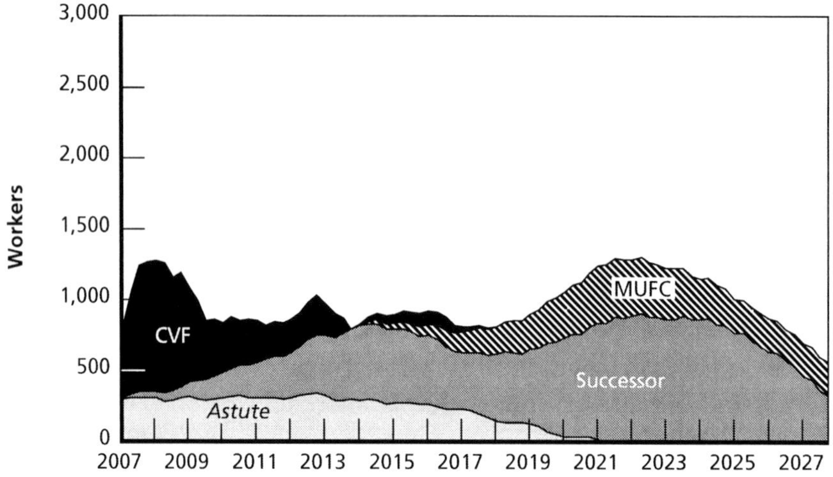

RAND *MG725-5.8*

a steady demand of around 800 workers, with two sharp peaks in 2008 and 2012 that approach 1,300 and 1,000 workers, respectively, before CVF demand falls as that programme completes and the demand of the future submarine programmes increase.

Demand for Detailed Designers and Professional Engineers

Our next stage of modelling at greater detail is to consider separately the two families of skills that together represent the technical workforce: detailed designers and professional engineers. In presenting these in the following figures, it is important to remember that we caveat the ability to interchange the use of a technical skill across the phases in the design and build processes. Our model and the supporting data do not distinguish between these processes or phases. Consequently, as we investigate demand in ever greater detail, there is a danger of an implied level of confidence or sense of precision. This is not intended, and we strive to describe the variations in demand while acknowledging that they may mask important, fundamental subtleties in the employment of these technical skills.

The value of analysis at this level of detail is to see if any general observations can be made about MOD programme demand on the detailed designer and professional engineer technical skill families.

Demand for Detailed Designers. Detailed design skills are used mostly in the design process and so these skills will be in greatest demand in the earlier stages of a vessel's programme. This is seen in Figure 5.9, with the peak demand for detailed designers arising earlier than peak demand for the technical workforce, shown in Figure 5.5, and the direct workforce, shown in Figure 5.1.

In this figure, the vertical axis has been scaled down to allow closer examination of the model output. CVF demand dominates in the early years, causing a maximum demand of about 1,050 workers. A trough occurs between 2009 and 2011 as detailed designers are less involved in the build processes for the CVF, *Astute*, and Type 45 programmes that are in progress at that point. A second period of high demand follows

Figure 5.9
Technical Detailed Designer Workforce Demand, by Ship Class

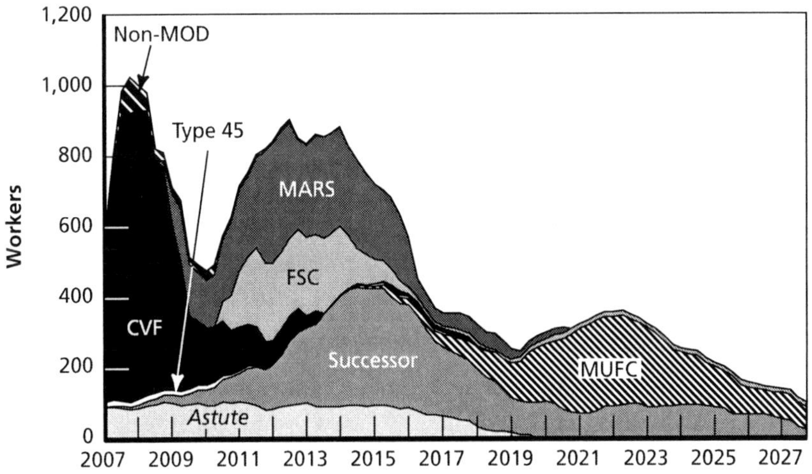

RAND *MG725-5.9*

until about 2016, when the design processes for MARS,[7] FSC, Successor, and MUFC overlap, decreasing until 2019, when a low level of support is required for the build processes of Successor and FSC. MUFC design work increases demand to about 350 workers in 2022. Again, comparing this demand to the information provided by our respondents and presented in Table 4.1 in Chapter Four, we see that the total detailed designer workforce is 998, with 457 in the surface and submarine groups. As we discuss elsewhere in this monograph, there is no Type 45 replacement programme in the baseline data. Consequently, there is no increase in demand for detailed designers around 2025–2030 as might otherwise be expected to ensure that a new class of ships is ready to replace the Type 45.

Demand for Professional Engineers and Technical Managers. Professional engineer and technical manager skills are used throughout the design and build processes. In Figure 5.10, which has an extended vertical axis, we can see how demand for these skills is spread more evenly than that for detailed designers, although there is a notably high demand from the Successor programme. There is a series of peaks in the first 15 years, with the MARS programme making a maximum demand of about 1,700 workers in 2013–2015. Demand in the later years, moving to the right in the figure, is again due to MARS (1,350 workers, 2019–2021) followed by the combined effect of the FSC, MUFC, and Successor programmes (1,200 workers, 2021–2027), though it is Successor demand that dominates. Overall, these peaks are caused by the cumulative, varying demands of the majority of MOD programmes, combined with those of non-MOD programmes that represent military export orders. The shape of the graph in this figure is similar to other figures in this chapter, showing total technical demand and total labour demand. Respondents to our survey reported 2,527 professional engineers with 1,599 in the surface ship and submarine groups.

---

7 Because we are considering demand split by skill family rather than surface ship or submarine programme, we include MARS in this discussion. In the next chapter, we look at the vessel programmes and skill families separately and MARS will be excluded. Retention here and in the next section allows discussion of the potential impact of that programme.

Figure 5.10
Technical Professional Engineer and Technical Manager Workforce Demand, by Ship Class

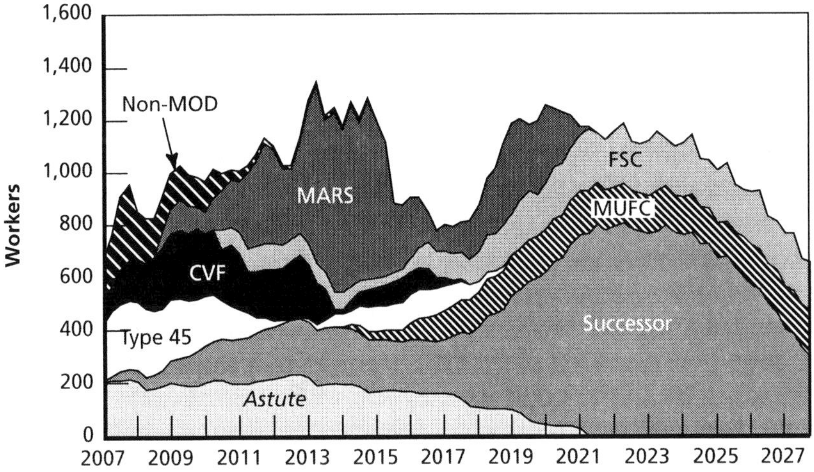

RAND *MG725-5.10*

Observations

Based on the data presented in this chapter, we are able to make the following observations:

- *The total labour demand from MOD's future shipbuilding programme in the next eight years is double the long-term demand; however, submarine workforce demands are constant. The CVF programme is the major contributor to near-term complex surface ship demand.* The overall potential future demand for the entire programme will reach a peak around 2013.[8] The complex surface ship programme demand is dominated by CVF in the near term with considerably lower labour requirements in the longer term. Indeed, CVF places such an increased demand on the industry

[8] We say *potential* because the MIS identifies only certain parts of the overall programme as the core workload that is committed to delivery onshore.

for a short, notable period that it exacerbates the size of the reduction in the long-term steady demand represented by the FSC programme. The submarine programme at the total labour demand level is stable.

- *Overall, technical workforce demands generally mirror those of the total workforce.* However, technical skills are generally used in the earlier stages of the design and build processes of maritime vessel programmes. CVF is again a dominant programme, distorting complex surface ship demand and delaying the decline to the long-term steady state represented by the FSC programme. If it is included, MARS again has a dramatic impact on demand, while the submarine programme is generally stable but with increasing demand in the 2020–2026 time frame.
- *Although highly variable, demand for detailed designer technical skills is constantly reduced in the short term before significantly reducing after 2017.* From a current high, detailed designer demand may be considered relatively constant at around 600–800 workers until about 2015, although the exact level will depend on the extent to which design efforts for different MARS ship classes are conducted onshore. A Type 45 replacement programme, which is not currently planned by MOD, would likely increase demand to FSC levels, though this would not be until later in the period under investigation and there would be a long gap of negligible demand.
- *Demand for total professional engineer technical skills is relatively constant, notwithstanding the requirements of the MARS programme.* Total professional engineer technical demand from the MOD programme is relatively stable over the next 15 years, except for labour required by MARS programme. If this is included, the demand surges considerably, which may present a mid-term challenge to the MOD.

CHAPTER SIX

Demand for Individual Technical Skills Generated by MOD Current Complex Surface Ship and Submarine Programmes

In this chapter, we provide the results of our analysis of demand for individual technical skills generated by all complex surface ships and submarines in MOD's build programme. These are the individual skills defined in Chapter Three.

As seen earlier, the technical skills fall into two major subsets—detailed design and professional engineering. When analysing the demands on individual technical skills, we found that the resulting profiles mostly followed the same general trend within each of these family subsets.[1] Thus, to portray our analysis results, in this chapter, we present one technical skill from each family. This allows for easier comparison and enables us to maintain some consistency of analysis. There are some anomalies amongst the individual skills, and we show an example of this, too, to highlight the strength of our modelling tool and reinforce the value of investigating demand at the technical skill level.

For the detailed designer family, we present the future workload demand for the electrical and control skill set (dubbed DD E&C for our purposes in this chapter); for the professional engineer family, our representative skill is mechanical/fluids (dubbed PE M/E). Estimated demand graphs for each of the individual technical skills, modelled

[1] One notable exception to this is testing, commissioning, and acceptance professional engineers; the major activities for this skill tend to occur at the end of the build cycle. However, in our interviews with industry personnel, we heard that many of the personnel in this skill set are multiskilled and have the ability to work in other areas; this mitigates against the peakiness of the graph in Figure D.10 in Appendix D.

at the complex surface ship and submarine levels (respectively) can be found in Appendix D.[2]

In this chapter, we examine the estimated demand for our representative individual technical skills (DD E&C and PE M/E) under three conditions:

- demand from all MOD programmes
- demand from MOD complex surface ship programmes
- demand from MOD submarine programmes.

Demand for Individual Skills from All MOD Programmes

The first step is to consider the combined demand of MOD's maritime programmes on our chosen representative skills. This will give a better perspective of the demand of the separate categories that we consider later in this chapter: complex surface ship programmes and submarine programmes.

Detailed Designer Demand at the Individual Skill Level

We saw in Chapter Five how demand for detailed designers in the design process caused earlier peaks of maximum demand. This is shown again in Figure 6.1, in which only the DD E&C skill is shown.

The combined demand of MOD's programmes is uneven, with several sharp peaks corresponding to the commencement of new programmes. Initially, CVF pushes demand to about 230 workers in 2008, with a sharp decrease to about 120 in 2010. A second sharp peak occurs in 2013–2015 as the FSC design process increases demand on top of that for Successor and MARS. Not surprisingly, this figure is very similar to Figure 5.9 in Chapter Five, which shows total detailed designer

---

[2] An additional question that may arise from this analysis is what level of technical staff should be retained, by skill, to most cost-effectively meet future demand peaks. Although this question was not explicitly addressed in this research, previous RAND work on the U.S. submarine design base suggests a rough rule that the minimum level for retention should be between one-third and one-half of the future demand peak. The exact level will vary, depending on the skill and how immediate the future peak of demand is.

Figure 6.1
Technical Labour Demand for Detailed Designer Electrical and Control Skill, All Programmes

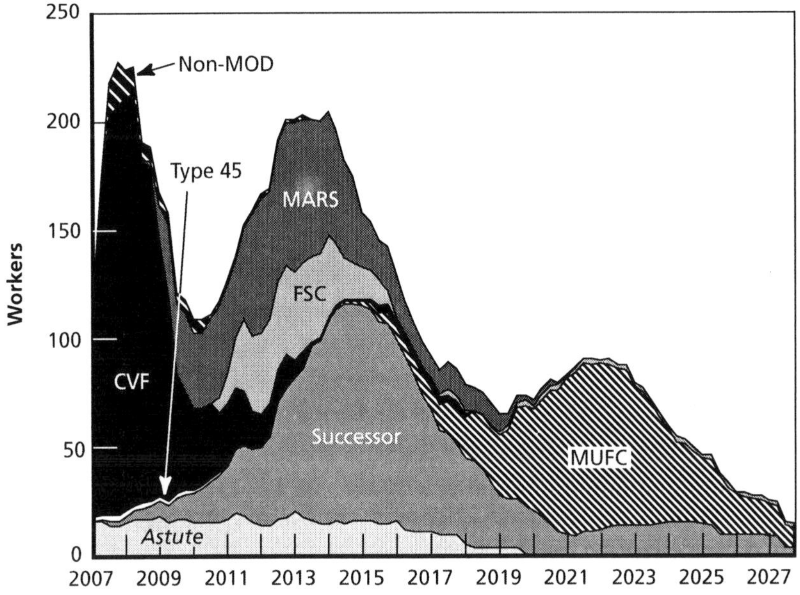

RAND *MG725-6.1*

demand for these programmes. From Table 4.1 we see that our survey respondents reported 210 DD E&C workers split across the design/build and support groups; there are 96 workers in the design/build group.

Professional Engineer Demand at the Individual Skill Level

Repeating this process for our chosen PE M/F skill, we get the demand shown in Figure 6.2; this should be compared with Figure 5.10, which shows demand for all professional engineer skills.

This skill shows less correlation to that earlier all-skill graph, suggesting that there are more significant differences in demand across the professional engineer skills than seen in detailed designers. Deductively, this might be linked to the larger number of skills modelled (four detailed designer, eight professional engineer), a divergence of use of these skills in the design and build processes that is not true for detailed

Figure 6.2
Technical Labour Demand for Professional Engineer Mechanical/Fluids Skill, All Programmes

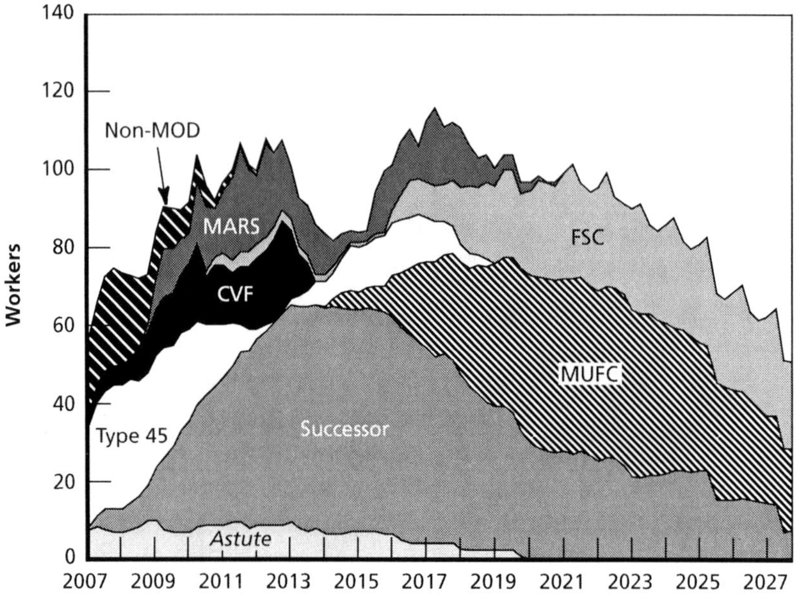

RAND *MG725-6.2*

designers (who are predominant in just the design process), or a combination of both these reasons.

Closer examination of Figures 6.2 and 5.10 does allow some correlation to be identified; for example, it is apparent that demand from the MARS programme for this skill is less and more even than that seen for all the professional engineer skills together. For the PE M/F skill, there is a steady demand of about 90 workers for the next 20 years. There are some occasional peaks and troughs as the different vessel programmes pick up or draw down, but these are the least dramatic variations of any skill or collection of skills we modelled. There are 174 workers for this skill in Table 4.1, with 89 in the design/build group.[3]

---

[3] Remember that we repeat the numbers from Table 4.1 to give a better perspective on projected demand. It was not part of our study to undertake supply and demand analysis.

Demand for Individual Skills from Complex Surface Ship Programmes

Detailed Designer Demand at the Individual Skill Level

We first look at the DD E&C future labour requirements for complex surface ships.[4] Figure 6.3 shows this demand.

This figure shows a near-term upsurge in the requirement for these detailed designers, followed by a short trough in 2010 before a continuing broad peak requirement during the first-of-class design process for FSC. Demand then falls to practically zero in 2016. This is because there is no requirement for a new future warship design until a Type 45 replacement is needed. This is unlikely to happen much before the early

Figure 6.3
Technical Labour Demand for Detailed Designer Electrical and Control Skill, Complex Surface Ship Programmes

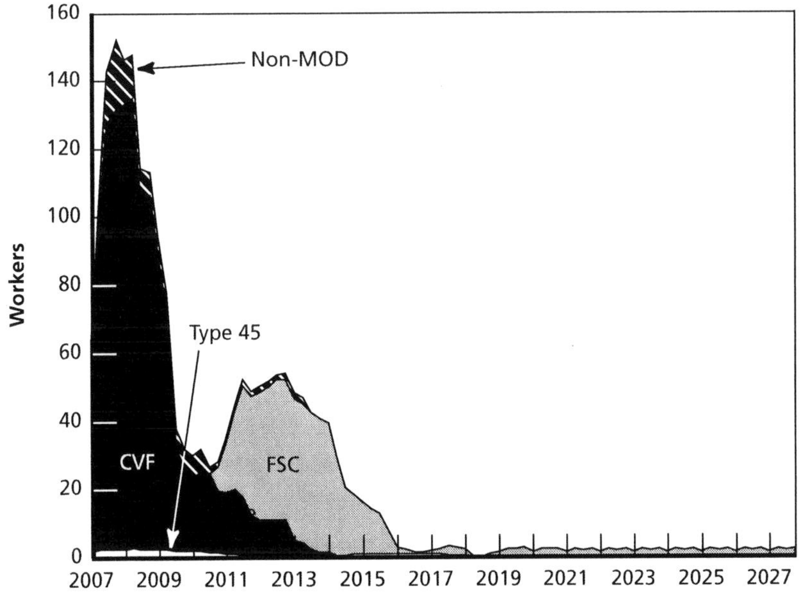

RAND *MG725-6.3*

[4] Because a portion of CVF is planned to be designed and built in a traditional submarine yard, we have reduced the design effort accordingly in the following analysis.

to mid-2020s, leading to an extended gap in demand. Similar patterns are present for all the detailed designer skills, as can be seen in Figures D.1–D.3 and D.13–D.15 in Appendix D. Unsurprisingly, there are variations in demand for the different skills, but, overall, an extended gap in demand exists from 2016, and this will last until the start of work on the Type 45 replacement. A gap in demand of this duration suggests that it will be difficult to sustain the detailed designer skills without adjusting programmes or through other methods of intervention.

Professional Engineer Demand at the Individual Skill Level

The demand for PE M/F is different. Figure 6.4 shows the estimated future complex surface ship demand for this skill.

Figure 6.4
Technical Labour Demand for Professional Engineer Mechanical/Fluids Skill, Complex Surface Ship Programmes

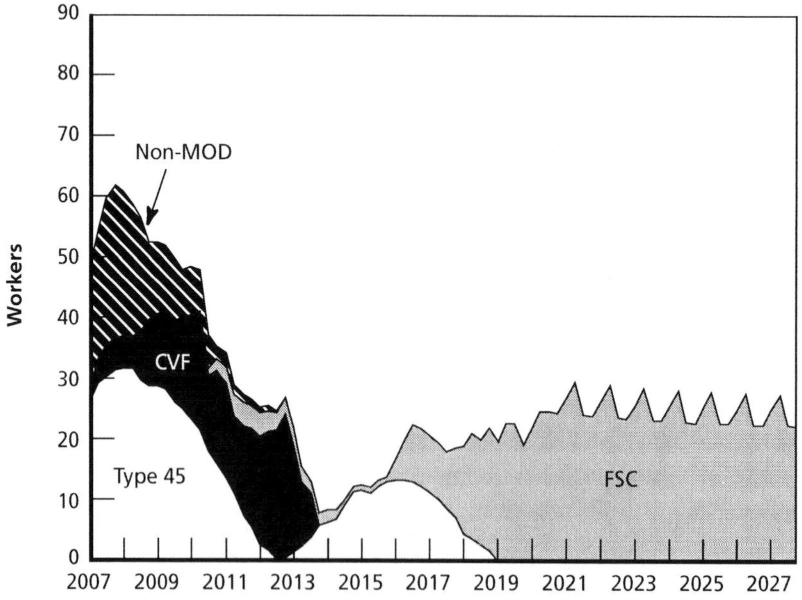

RAND *MG725-6.4*

After a broad near-term peak arising from support to Type 45, CVF, and non-MOD programmes,[5] demand decreases sharply until 2014. At that point, demand increases as the last two Type 45 hulls are completed and the build process for FSC picks up. After 2017, the FSC programme provides long-term steady demand for this skill. Figures D.4–D.10 and D.16–D.21 in Appendix D show a similar pattern of demand for the other professional engineer skills. Thus, compared to detailed design skills in the complex ship sector, demand for professional engineering skills is more constant, although there may need to be interventions to sustain these skills over the 2013–2017 period. Although the level of many of the skills is more constant, industry and MOD will also need to ensure that the complexity of such work sustains the skills. For example, combat systems technical requirements for complex warships, such as Type 45 and FSC, may be more demanding than those for ships such as CVF and MARS and may require additional measures to sustain specific aspects of combat systems and integration skills.

Demand for Individual Skills from Submarine Programmes

Detailed Designer Demand at the Individual Skill Level

Figure 6.5 shows the DD E&C demand from MOD's submarine programmes.

Demand for this skill increases ever more quickly until reaching a peak around 2015 of about 120 workers. It then descends sharply to a trough close to 55 in 2019 before peaking again at 90 workers in 2022. Demand on this skill is heavily influenced by the expected sharp demand in support of the design process of Successor between 2010 and 2019. MUFC design process demand starts in 2014 and initially

---

[5] Due to the nature of the work, this non-MOD export-order demand estimate is available only for the short term. It is possible that it will continue to be a key component of the professional engineering demand going forward, but that is not assured. Thus, we included it only in the short-term analysis, so as not to overestimate these levels.

Figure 6.5
Technical Labour Demand for Detailed Designer Electrical and Control Skill, Submarine Programmes

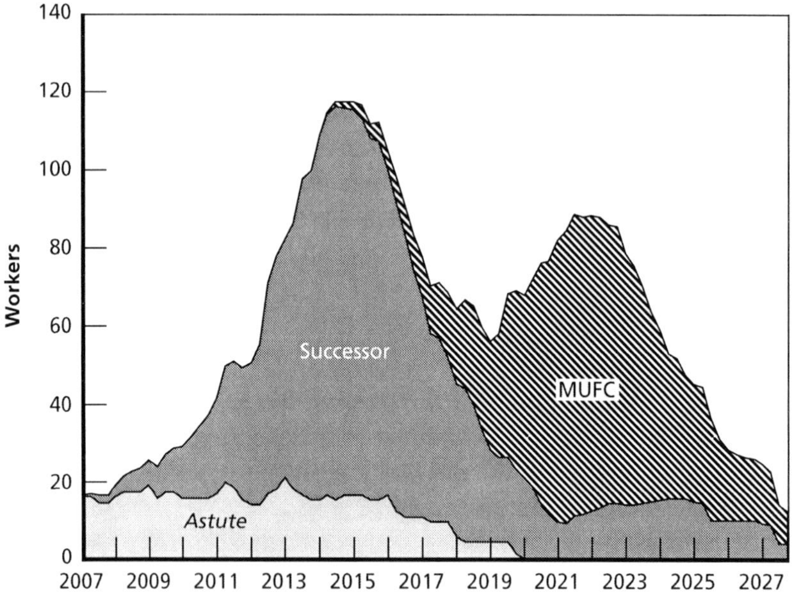

RAND *MG725-6.5*

compounds this effect to produce the total peak of about 115 workers. There is little build process demand for this skill.

As discussed in Chapter Five, MOD demand at the submarine shipyard will include elements of the CVF programme. We show the addition of the CVF element to the submarine programme in Figure 6.6. This, then, is the demand on that skill at the submarine yard.

As can be seen, the CVF-element design process and the *Astute* programme build process combine to place a peak demand on this skill in 2008 of approximately 80 workers. The demand decreases as CVF work tails off, until the increasing demand of the Successor design process rapidly picks up to the peak shown in Figure 6.5. There are two areas that may require intervention if this skill is to be sustained at a steady level during the period under investigation. First, there is a dip in demand between 2009 and 2013. Second, early design activity for the MUFC programme around 2017 is insufficient until 2020 to pick up

Figure 6.6
Technical Labour Demand for Detailed Designer Electrical and Control Skill in the Submarine Sector with CVF Demand Included

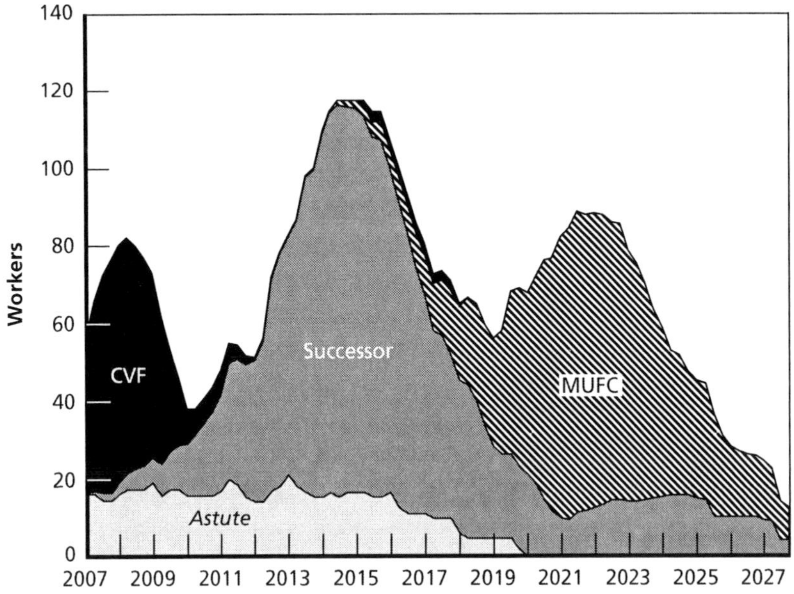

RAND *MG725-6.6*

demand as that for Successor decreases. Subsequently, there is a significant fall as the MUFC programme moves to production.

Professional Engineer Demand at the Individual Skill Level

Figure 6.7 shows future demand for the PE M/F skill as steadily increasing in the near term to a very broad peak of around 65–75 workers from 2013 to 2023. This increase is due initially to the design process of the Successor programme, to which is added the early design work for MUFC. As Successor moves toward the build process, demand from that programme decreases quickly, but overall demand reduces more slowly as the MUFC design process places greater demand on the skill.

In Figure 6.8, we repeat our method of comparison by inclusion of the demand of the CVF element. For CVF, demand for the PE M/F skill is more even through the design and build processes. The effect

Figure 6.7
Technical Labour Demand for Professional Engineer Mechanical/Fluids Skill in the Submarine Sector

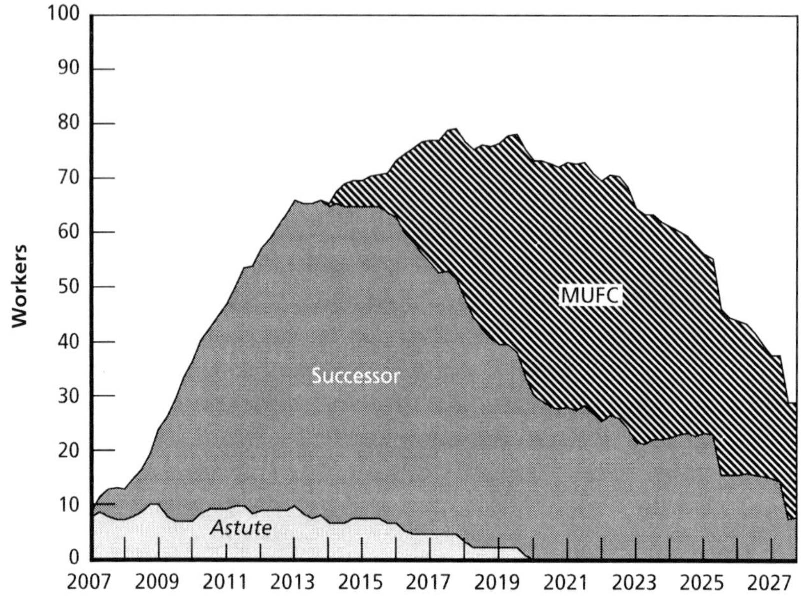

RAND *MG725-6.7*

is to compound the rising Successor demand to produce a sharp peak around 2012 of about 85 workers.

For the professional engineer skills overall, it appears that demand continues downward beyond 2027.

Observations

Based on the data presented in this chapter, we are able to make the following observations:

- *Without additional work, it will be difficult to sustain detailed design skills after completion of the design process for FSC.* There are only two warship programmes which significantly contribute to individual detailed design skills—CVF and FSC. After around

Figure 6.8
Technical Labour Demand for Professional Engineer Mechanical/Fluids Skill in the Submarine Sector with CVF Demand Included

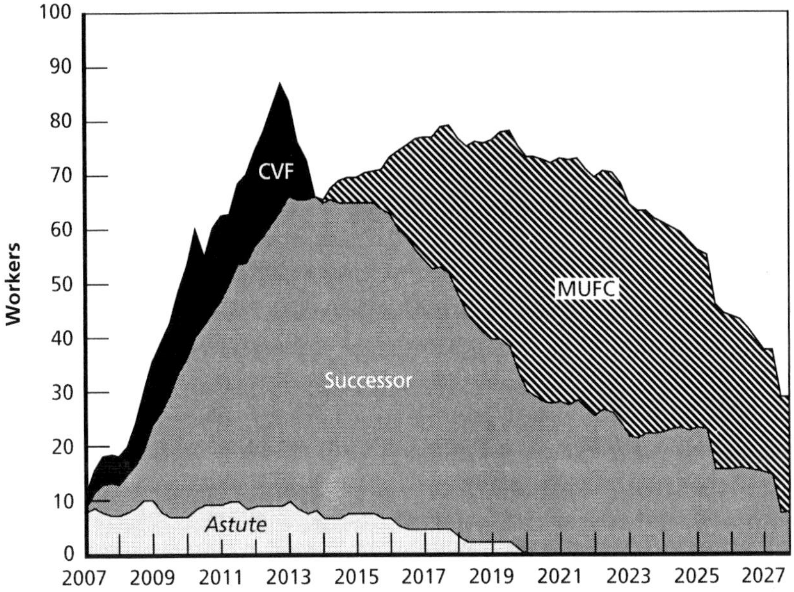

RAND *MG725-6.8*

2015, there will be little demand for these skills until a potential Type 45 replacement design begins in the early to mid-2020s. Demand from the design process for the later ships in the MARS programme may offer some mitigation, but this will impact not only detailed design skills, but those of professional engineers as well.

- *There is steady demand on professional engineering skills from MOD's complex warship programmes.* An initial peak in demand from CVF is followed by a trough as that programme concludes and the final hulls of the Type 45 programme are completed. FSC then provides a constant demand. The full MARS programme may overload demand for some skills.
- *The CVF programme provides a bridge for both submarine detailed design and professional engineering skills prior to the start of the Successor new design.* There is a lack of demand for most individual

technical skills if the CVF programme is not included. However, once it is added to demand, it sustains individual technical skills, particularly those of detailed designers, until the Successor programme picks up.

- *The start of the MUFC programme at the peak caused by Successor demand exacerbates total demand and the subsequent decline in demand.* MOD may need to investigate options for smoothing this peak demand, for example, by amending the timing of the MUFC programme.

CHAPTER SEVEN

Key Findings

Looking at this analysis more broadly, some general trends emerge with regard to the future demand for design and engineering technical skills in both the submarine and surface ship sectors. We present these with commentary to support each key point.

- *The MOD baseline programme will need some modification to help sustain the technical skills that support the key industrial capabilities. The nature of the modification and its implementation requires further investigation.* The current MOD baseline programme will not sustain all of the technical skills needed to support the future maritime programme. Within the complex warship and submarine sectors, there are periods of low activity (such as a lack of work for detailed designers post–FSC design) which will not sustain those technical skills. MOD has aspirations to undertake other maritime programmes and these, or elements of them, may help mitigate gaps in demand that exist under current plans. Even so, some technical skills may require targeted initiatives if they are to be sustained.
- *Overall, there is sufficient demand from the submarine programmes to sustain design and build submarine technical skills until 2027, although beyond this, the situation is less clear.* There are no gaps in technical labour demand from design/build submarine programmes for the next 15 years. The difficulty in this period will be to be to manage the increases in skills needed to deliver the Successor and MUFC programmes; professional engineering demand ramps up significantly and will require rapid assimilation of new

workers. There is a downturn in detailed design labour requirements after 2022, when the design efforts of these programmes conclude. This will pose longer-term problems should no further design work arise. Professional engineering demand peaks around 2018 and steadily declines as first Successor and then MUFC near completion. The relationship between the end of these programmes and the start of any future submarine programmes will affect the demand that will sustain these skills. The CVF programme serves a valuable bridging function in the near term by providing additional workload to both the detailed design and professional engineer technical skills at the submarine shipyard. Within the support sector, the demand on technical skills is much more variable

- *The complex surface ship sector is more fragile than the submarine base when looking at design/build technical skills.* Demand for detailed design skills varies greatly in the near term and, following the FSC first-of-class design work around 2012–2016, there is little future activity to sustain these skills until the start of a Type 45 replacement programme. For the professional engineering community, the demand is more constant, although there are periods of lesser demand that may need intervention.[1] Should MOD decide to change the maritime surface programme and trigger, for example, reductions in new hull numbers, gaps in demand for professional engineering skills will develop quickly and may become difficult to sustain. MOD intervention would then be necessary to mitigate the impact of such decisions. However, when one examines the support programme, the demand on technical skills in the complex surface ship sector is much more steady.
- *A specific maritime programme demand sustains detailed design and professional engineering technical skills in different ways.* Detailed designers are in most demand during the design process of first-

[1] For example, in the period between CVF and FSC production from 2013 to 2017. Within these periods of lower demand, MOD will need to ensure that its potential interventions sustain all of its key technical skills. Some skills, such as combat systems, may not be exercised as greatly by the inclusion of simpler RFA-type ships.

of-class ships or submarines. Professional engineers are involved more equally across the design and build processes, but demand varies for any given hull and between successive hulls. Both sets of skills work together during the design process, and demand for one invariably affects the other. Specific steps to sustain detailed designers, for example, could increase demand on professional engineers already employed in other activities.

- *Examining MOD labour demand requirements at different levels of aggregation highlights different trends and challenges.* By looking at labour demand at a variety of levels (total labour, technical labour, detailed design/professional engineer, and individual skills), different trends are revealed. This ability is important, as it allows those making decisions on the future shipbuilding programme to better understand how they might affect the maritime industry. For example, examining technical labour in aggregate helps MOD understand general labour requirements and whether there is a general lack of demand (as there is in complex ship detailed design skills), while modelling at the individual skill level provides insight into how bespoke intervention may generate sufficient demand to sustain those skills at risk.
- *There is a need to review technical labour demand requirements as programme assumptions change.* When conducting sensitivity analysis, we examined how changes to the MOD programme could affect the demand needed to sustain technical skills. Changes which may be made to solve one problem may exacerbate another. MOD now has the tools necessary to understand some of the industrial consequences of changes to the maritime programme. These tools will also aid longer-term planning.
- *Recruiting certain technical skill sets will be challenging for industry.* Our industry interviews and survey highlighted the challenges of recruiting technical staff of the appropriate skill type and experience. Specifically, respondents highlighted difficulties finding experienced professional engineers who were naval architects, electrical (power) engineers, systems engineers, and mechanical engineers.

- *As processes develop and technologies mature, the required mix of technical skills will change.* Those technical skills needed today may not be required in the future. In our interviews and survey responses, industry anticipates increasing requirements for IT skills and electrical engineers. Working practices are also forecast to change leading to, for example, greater remote working and a need for wider language skills. Again, MOD may wish to engage with industry to stay attuned to these trends so that its industrial strategy can sustain the skills that will be needed in the future.

CHAPTER EIGHT

Areas for Further Investigation

The key findings in Chapter Seven may generate discussion and questions that lead to the need for further analysis. In addition, there are several areas of further investigation which stand out and that MOD may wish to consider. The purpose of this chapter is to signpost how a better understanding might be gained of the relationships between technical skills and MOD's maritime programme demand.

- *Add support/repair/refit data to the labour demand forecasting model as information becomes available.* In this phase of research, shipyards that conduct repair/refit activities on behalf of MOD were not able to provide future labour demand data by skill at the level of detail that was required. To compensate for this, we describe an alternative strategy in Appendix A to estimate this future support demand. However, should labour demand data become available to the degree of granularity required, MOD should look to integrate this with the existing model data. This would allow subsequent analysis to gain a clearer understanding of any potential symbiotic relationships among design, production, and support resources and could help MOD to model potential changes across the maritime lifespan of its fleet, should the future programme change.
- *Further investigate how MOD demand sustains key equipment suppliers.* This study focussed on understanding how demand sus-

tains technical skills primarily at the shipyard level.[1] However, shipyards utilise subcontractors and other key suppliers to provide key pieces of equipment and integration activities. By examining how demand affects each of these in a more systematic way, MOD can better understand where any risks in sustaining this level of supply could occur and develop strategies to mitigate them.

- *Examine in greater depth MOD's technical skills requirement to gain a deeper understanding of the technical base that is needed to meet the MOD's internal needs.* Although this research provides insights into the technical skills present in industry which the forward programme should look to sustain, MOD also has a responsibility to ensure that its own technical staff has the skills required to plan, execute, and monitor its future programme. This includes ensuring that the right mix of technical skills exists within the ministry and that those skills are used and developed appropriately. This will ensure that MOD remains an "intelligent buyer" and is able to understand the technical aspects of its future requirements.
- *Conduct further analysis on those technical skills whose low population numbers may not have been fully considered during this level of modelling.* When conducting our modelling activity, we defined the technical skill categories at a level at which it would be possible to estimate future demand meaningfully. However, our survey work identified some technical skills that would be difficult to quantitatively model because of their low population numbers and niche capabilities. These technical skills may be important to the future MOD programme and should be examined in more depth to provide greater understanding of their importance in maintaining the key industrial capabilities required by the MIS. An initial assessment of these niche skills can be found in Appendix B.
- *Continue to assess potential changes to the MOD future programme to understand threats to the ability to sustain key technical skill populations.* As the future MOD maritime programme develops, it is important to ensure that any proposed changes take into account

---

1 And at the associated first-tier supply level.

the need to sustain key technical skills. To do this, MOD must continue to understand the impact of its maritime programme on these skills and keep its analytical tools updated so that changes can be assessed.

- *Investigate ways to sustain technical skills in periods of insufficient demand.* The extent to which the MOD shipbuilding programme may be manipulated will be affected by the operational requirements of the Royal Navy and the RFA, as well as the resources available to the maritime portion of the equipment plan. Consequently, there may be no alternative but for some skills to be underused in normal shipbuilding programmes for extended periods, placing them under threat. There are likely to be a number of potential solutions to this problem. In the immediate future, however, because of the anticipated demand, it is unlikely that any skills will become critical, and so MOD and industry have a window in which to investigate and put in place an agreed upon solution or series of solutions.
- *Understand how technical skills might change with advances in process or the introduction of new technologies.* It is likely that there will continue to be advances in the way in which ships and submarines are designed, built, and supported. This has been seen recently, for example, in the changes to the nuclear submarine design and build processes for the *Astute* and *Virginia* classes. If there are long gaps between successive demands, the sustaining activity placed by MOD to maintain current capability and capacity could entrench existing processes at the expense of allowing the development or inclusion of new processes and the skills to support them.

APPENDIX A

Incorporating Support, Repair/Refit, and Other Labour into the Shipyard Labour Modelling Tool

In Chapter Five, we discussed why our quantitative modelling activity did not include support activities. Because industry data were not available by individual skill category from the firms that undertake support activities,[1] we were not able to model their data to the same degree of granularity with which the rest of the labour demand data were presented.

In this appendix, we present a methodology and assumptions that allow us to incorporate these support data into our wider modelling outputs. However, since the data does not originate in a "like-for-like" format, we did not include them in the main body of this monograph. However, there are three sources of data which, when combined with a number of assumptions, can help us estimate and integrate technical labour support requirements into our wider data set. They are

- MOD estimates of the production workforce required for future support activities
- MOD estimates of specific technical workforce requirements for those firms involved in MOD's Design Support Alliance (DSA) activities
- previous RAND work on the UK naval shipbuilding industrial base, which shows ratios of technical labour requirements to production work.

[1] Available from only one firm, and not by activity—only by total aggregate technical labour.

MOD does not appear to capture future labour demand projections for the technical workforce in the support sector; however, it does have models to estimate this future labour demand for production staff. These data are estimated by ship class and allow MOD to understand the future production labour requirements for the operational fleet.

In addition to holding estimates for production workforce labour demand, MOD also holds some data that estimate technical workforce requirements for those firms involved in its DSA. Industrial members of the DSA collaborate to meet MOD demand for design/support requirements for a subset of the wider support programme. These estimates can broadly broken down into detailed designer and professional engineer specialties, and roughly have a 5:2 (designer to engineer) ratio.

Previous RAND work on the UK naval shipbuilding industrial base also briefly addressed support activities.[2] This work estimated future MOD support activity demand and broke it down into five labour categories: management, technical, structural, outfitting, and support. For support activities, the technical labour component was approximately 25 percent of the overall support labour demand, and the labour profiles led the others by approximately six months.

Using these three data sources, we were able to construct a rough order-of-magnitude estimate for technical support labour requirements. We did this through three discrete steps. First, we estimated total technical labour demand over time. We did this by taking the total production workforce demand and, using previous production/technical labour ratios, we were able to estimate technical labour requirements. We then shifted these estimates forward in time (by two quarters) to account for the trend of technical labour profiles to lead other labour profiles by six months. Figure A.1 shows our estimate for total technical labour requirements for support activities (by major ship class).

Second, we took our new estimate for total technical support labour estimates and divided it into its two principle subcomponents. By using the DSA labour ratio of five detailed designers to two professional engineers, we were able to produce technical labour profile

---

[2] Arena et al. (2005).

Figure A.1
Estimated Technical Labour Profile for Support Activities

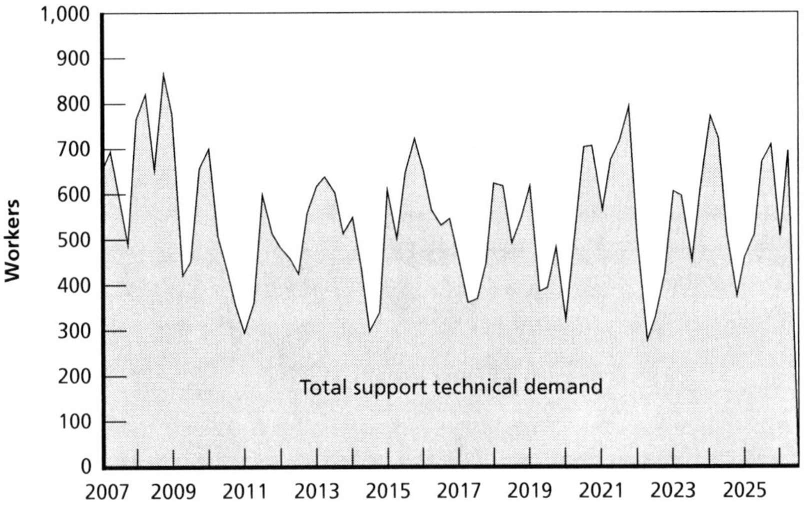

RAND *MG725-A.1*

estimates for these two categories. Figures A.2 and A.3 shows the labour profiles for these categories, respectively, by ship class.

Finally, we were able to integrate these two estimated profiles into the wider labour estimates for detailed designers and professional engineers, presented in Figures 5.7 and 5.8 in Chapter Five. This allows us to see the impact of support activities within the wider technical demand.

Figure A.4 shows that, although there appears to be greater short-term demand for detailed designers in the design/build component of labour demand, the long-term demand is more heavily weighted toward the support phase. This may be because some future design programmes, such as a Type 45 replacement, are not included in our modelling output.

In Figure A.5, we see that the level of technical support demand is considerably less than that required for the design/build portion of MOD's future programme. The large discrepancy between the two types of labour demand for professional engineering technical resources raises some questions about the assumptions used in producing the

Figure A.2
Estimated Labour Profiles for Detailed Designers, Support Activities

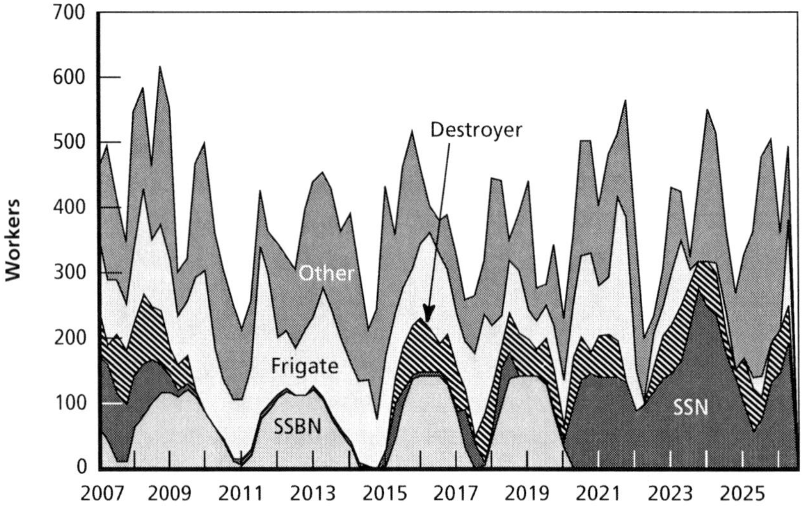

RAND *MG725-A.2*

Figure A.3
Estimated Labour Profiles for Professional Engineers, Support Activities

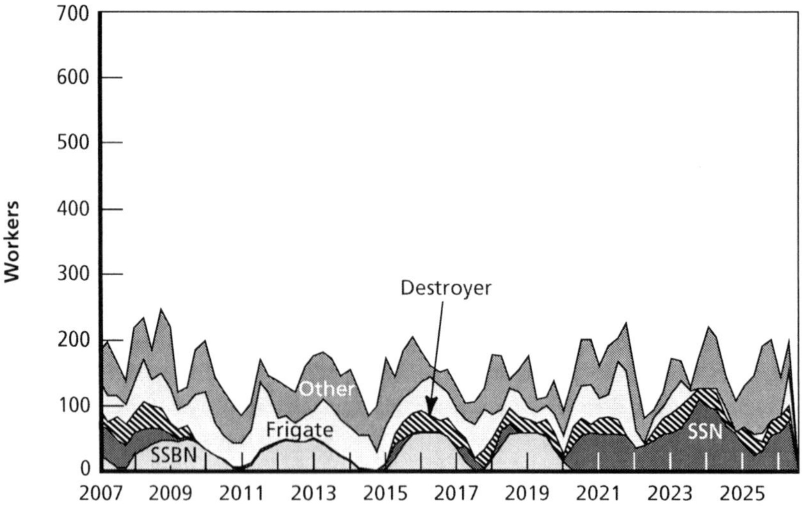

RAND *MG725-A.3*

Figure A.4
Integrating Support Estimates into Overall Detailed Designer Labour Projections

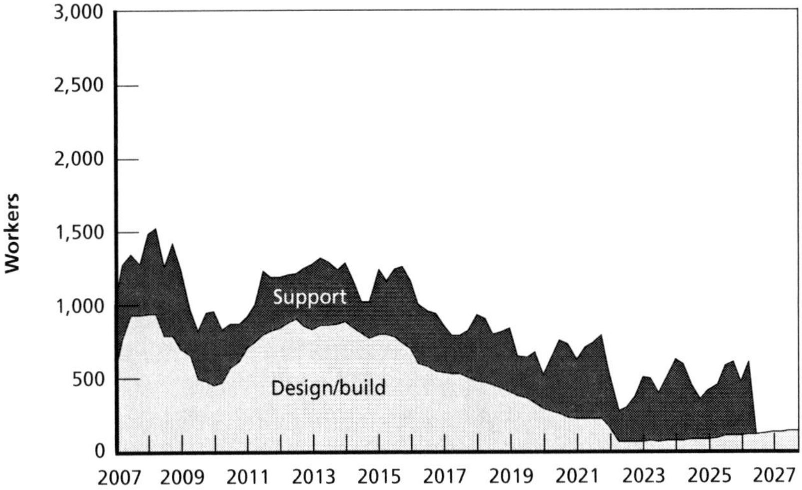

RAND *MG725-A.4*

Figure A.5
Integrating Support Estimates into Overall Professional Engineer Labour Projections

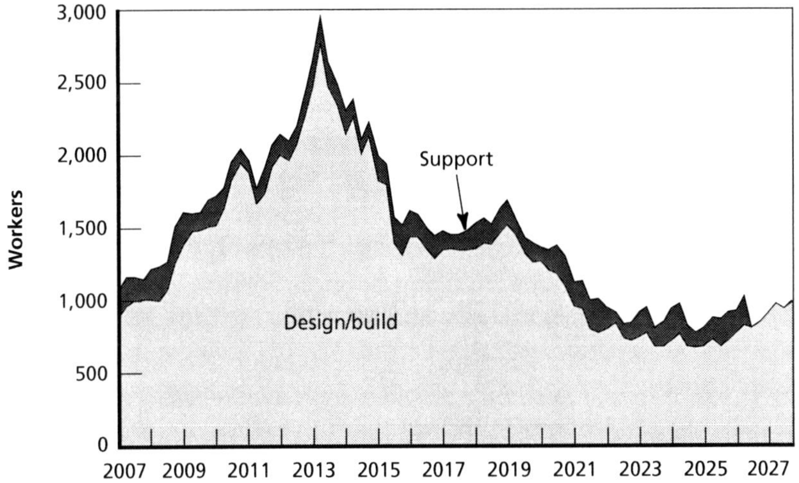

RAND *MG725-A.5*

support estimate. Further investigation is required to determine the source of this apparent discrepancy; however, this will not be possible until the support technical estimates are improved.

In summary, this appendix provided a methodology showing how MOD could estimate its future technical support activity labour requirements. We do not have the same level of confidence in the support estimates presented in the two preceding figures as in our projections presented in the main body of this monograph. However, they do give an illustration of the impact that support activities may have on MOD's overall technical workforce requirement.

APPENDIX B

Accounting for Low-Population, Highly Specialised Skills

The purpose of this research project was to help MOD understand how key skills contribute to the future UK maritime programme. To do this, we developed a list of key skills and, through data collected via surveys and interviews, assessed the impact of the future maritime programme on these skill sets. When defining the skills used in the research, we were forced to broadly define skills sets, as it would have been impractical and infeasible to model hundreds of different technical skills to the desired level of granularity. Thus, our skill definitions encompass a number of subskills that make up these broader skill sets. In Chapter Three, we showed (for example, in Figure 3.1) how this hierarchy was conceived. However, industry representatives stressed in our interviews that some skills were extremely important but comprised such small numbers of workers that they would be impractical to model using a quantitative method. It is important to note that many of these skills are contained in our skill categories; they are just subskills within the larger skill category. In this appendix, we report on those conversations with industry and present a list of those low-population, highly specialised skills, which MOD should monitor due to their importance in the delivery of the future programme.

When identifying these specific skills, it is necessary to understand the characteristics that make them both important to capture and difficult to quantitatively model. In general, these skills will likely include a combination of the following characteristics:

- risk of skill being lost within 10 years
- low population within MOD and industry

- highly specialised knowledge within skill set
- specific use within the ship/submarine design, build, or support phase
- not easily transferable or having a steep learning curve
- critical importance to future MOD design/platform
- limited fall-back option if skill depletes.

The UK Naval Engineering Science and Technology Forum (UK NEST) is a membership organisation which aims to facilitate discussion, promotion, and professional education regarding important naval technical skills and competencies. Membership in the forum is made up of key MOD maritime officials, as well as engineering directors and other key professionals in the UK maritime industry, and both platform design/build/support organisations and key suppliers are represented. Because these industry and MOD technical specialists best understand the challenges to define these specialised skills, we used the knowledge and expertise of UK NEST to capture these skills.

After presenting our initial research at one of the UK NEST meetings and having an in-depth discussion of the importance of these skills, forum members were invited to submit candidate skills to a central facilitator, who then screened them, shared the resulting list with senior colleagues for further insight, and provided the skill list to RAND. This skill list is wide in scope and cuts across the above- and underwater domains. The low-population, highly specialised skills are as follows:

- magnetic and electronic signatures
- submarine hydromechanics
- submarine nuclear propulsion
- pressure hull design
- sonar algorithm development
- alternative platform hullform design
- infrared signatures
- radar signatures
- surface platform survivability
- surface platform hydrodynamics and hydromechanics

- materials technology (including stealth composites)
- target strength modelling and measurement
- warship propulsion system integration
- weapon performance assessment
- cost engineering and estimation.

From the information provided for this part of our study, we make the following observations:

- In addition to considering the demand requirements placed on the general skill categories by the future maritime programme, MOD also needs to understand the impact of its programme on these low-population specialised skills. Should the existing programme not sustain them, MOD needs to explore with industry other means, such as technology demonstrators, periodic upgrades, or similar short-duration activities, to maintain these skills until they are needed again.
- Whilst this exercise was conducted only for key low-population skills, there would also be benefits in conducting a similar exercise for low-use, high-importance facilities.

APPENDIX C

RAND's Shipbuilding Modelling Tool

The goal of our modelling activity was to estimate future labour demands on specific skills for MOD's ship design, build, and support/repair/upgrade programme.[1] To do this, we followed a straightforward process. First, we developed a labour projection model that would allow us to estimate future demand. Second, in consultation with MOD, we made a set of basic assumptions concerning the future MOD maritime programme, including the timing and number of ships in a particular planned class (e.g., CVF, MARS, and FSC). Third, we collected demand data about these programmes from industry, MOD, and previous research and populated our labour projection model with that information. Finally, we ran the model to produce a number of estimates concerning the future labour demand of MOD programmes. Because the future maritime procurement plan is flexible and open to change, we also ran a number of other scenarios to look at the robustness of our projections.

The first step in our methodology was to develop a model that could accurately forecast future labour demands. The model used to project future MOD labour demand required a number of inputs. We show the model's general formulation in Figure C.1.

[1] For this research, we modified a RAND naval labour demand model that had been previously developed. The content of this appendix, explaining how the model works, has largely been taken largely from Arena et al. (2005).

Figure C.1
RAND's Basic Labour Forecasting Model

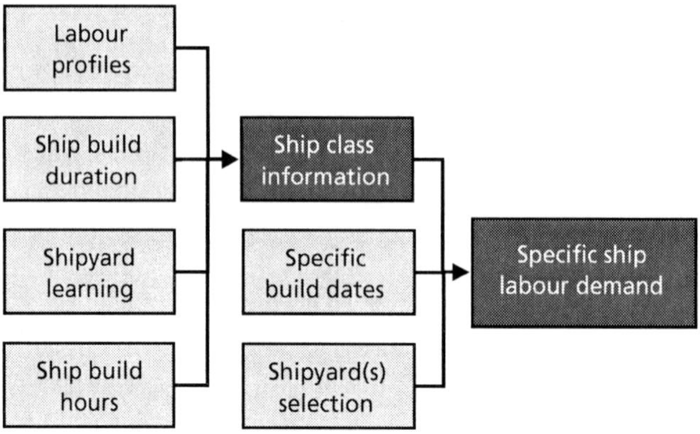

RAND *MG725-C.1*

The forecasting model requires data at a number of different levels. First, there is specific information associated with each ship class (e.g., Type 45, CVF). Such class-specific information includes

- *Labour profiles:* These profiles represent the distribution of labour required to build and design a ship over time. Although there may be a generic labour profile required for the overall production of a ship, it is also possible to estimate labour profiles for the individual skill trade areas associated with building a ship. In our model, we developed labour profiles unique to skill trade categories (which we will define later in this appendix).
- *Ship build hours:* These are the total number of direct worker hours required to complete a ship, which can be further broken down by individual skill trade areas (i.e., management, technical, structural, support, and outfitting).
- *Ship build duration:* This duration represents the total amount of time needed to actually build a ship. At this point in the modelling process, we did not identify specific start or stop dates for ship design or production, but instead made a general estimate of the overall block of time needed to build the ship (e.g., 10 quarters).
- *Shipyard learning curves:* These curves represent the labour hours required over time as more ships of the same class are produced.

> Improvement can come through increased labour proficiency, increased process innovation, or some combination of the two. Typical unit learning-curve slopes for shipbuilding range from 0.87 to 0.93,[2] and we used different learning curves depending on the ship class under consideration.

Past RAND studies have used this direct labour estimation model to assess overall labour demand. However, this study is primarily concerned with key technical skills, so we broke down overall labour into more definitive categories, making it possible to analyse demand at each of these levels.

Thus, for an individual ship class, it would then be possible to create representative, time-independent labour profiles for the number of direct workers required to design and produce a ship over time. We present a notional example of such profiles in Figure C.2.

However, to convert these notional labour projections into an actual estimate, two other important pieces of ship-specific information are required: Specific start and end dates for production need to be defined, and a specific shipyard(s) must be selected to actually design and produce the vessel. Only when these two steps are completed will the nominal labour projection shown in Figure C.2 be useful in estimating future labour demand for a specific naval vessel.

In our model, we made estimates for both these pieces of information. (We cover the specific information later in this appendix.)

As estimates are made for each future ship for the Royal Navy, it becomes possible to aggregate these individual estimates to come up with an overall labour estimate for the entire MOD shipbuilding programme. As mentioned before, these labour estimate aggregations can then be analysed at either a programme or skill level. We provide a visual representation of this aggregation in Figure C.3.

---

[2] By *unit learning-curve slope*, we mean the rate of improvement each time production doubles. A 0.95 slope, for example, means that the hours decrease by 5 percent each time the production unit doubles. It is a nonlinear improvement, getting smaller as the production quantity increases. See Mark V. Arena, John F. Schank, and Megan Abbott, *The Shipbuilding and Force Structure Analysis Tool: A User's Guide*, Santa Monica, Calif.: RAND Corporation, MR-1743-NAVY, 2004, for more details.

Figure C.2
Example of Direct Labour Distribution Curves for an Individual Ship Class

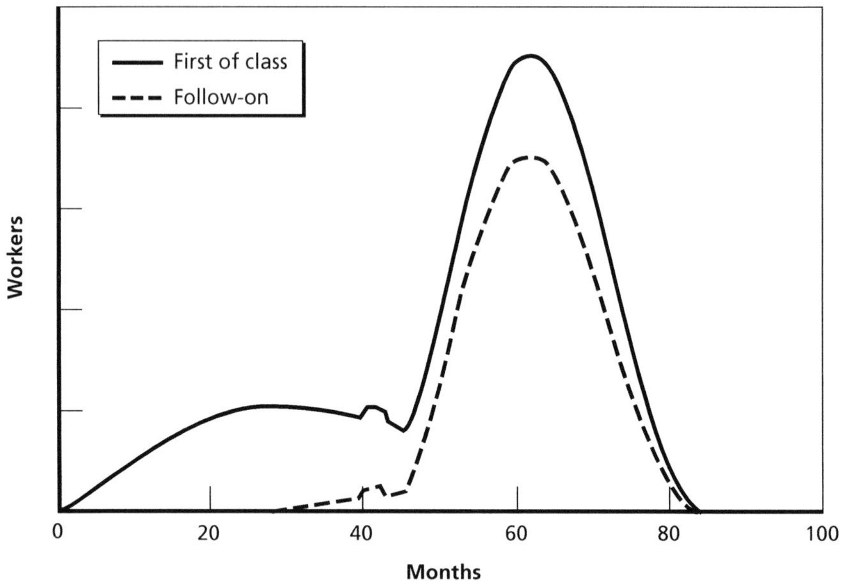

RAND *MG725-C.2*

Figure C.3
Individual Ship Aggregation to Represent Entire Shipbuilding Programme

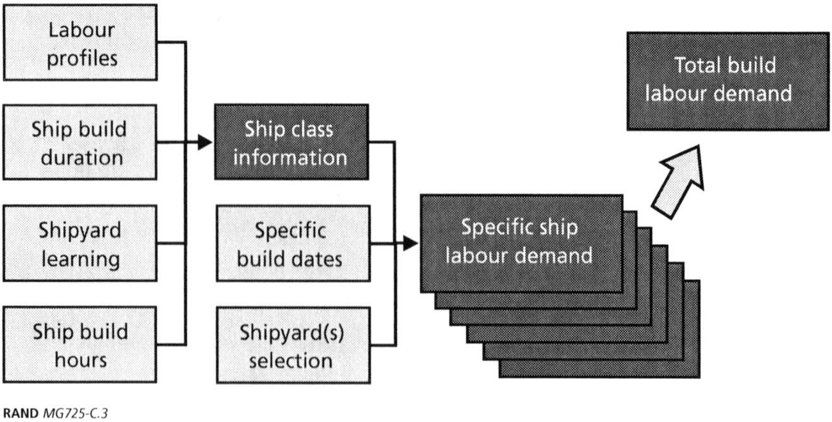

RAND *MG725-C.3*

APPENDIX D

Demand for Individual Technical Skills from MOD's Baseline Shipbuilding Programme

In Chapter Six, we discussed the impact of MOD's future shipbuilding programme on individual technical skills. To illustrate this impact, we chose to model two skills—detailed designer electrical and control and professional engineer mechanical/fluids—as a nearly representative sample of the larger set of individual skills. For completeness, we present the estimated future labour demand that the submarine and complex warship programmes, respectively, place on these technical skills.[1]

[1] For clarity, we have not included broad skills for which the figure would amalgamate a number of skills; for example, we have not included "other engineering" for either detailed designers or professional engineers. We also did not include any nuclear skills for complex surface ships, as the current fleet is conventionally powered.

Figure D.1
Demand from MOD Submarine Programmes for Detailed Designers—Electrical and Control

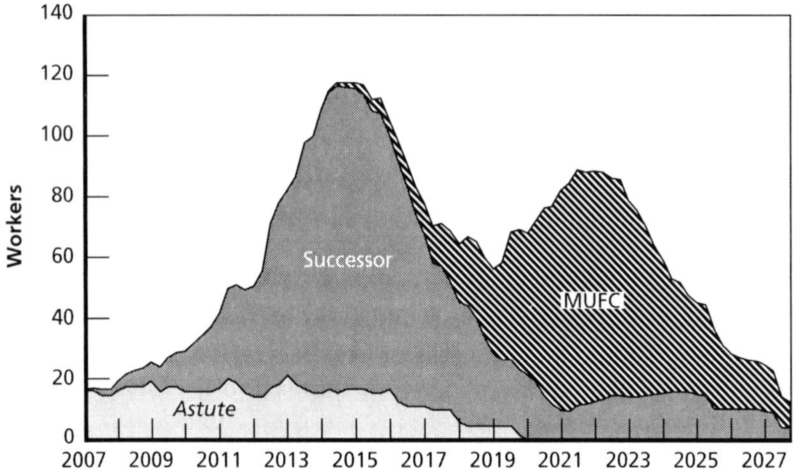

RAND *MG725-D.1*

Figure D.2
Demand from MOD Submarine Programmes for Detailed Designers—Mechanical/Fluids

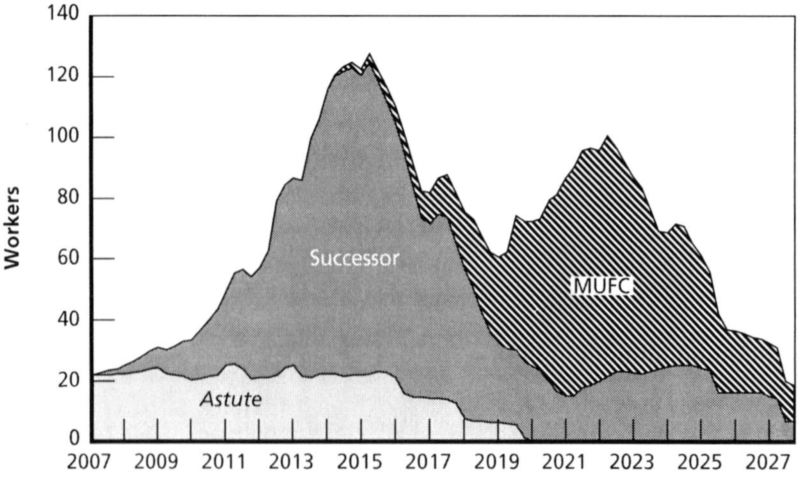

RAND *MG725-D.2*

Figure D.3
Demand from MOD Submarine Programmes for Detailed Designers—Hull/Structural/Arrangements

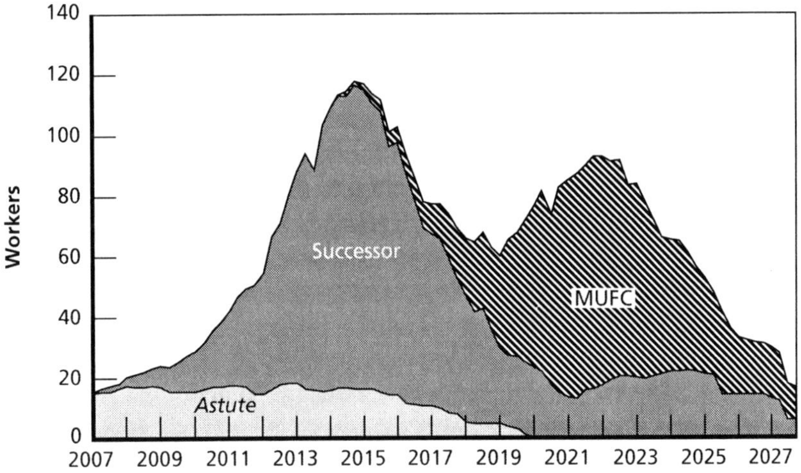

RAND *MG725-D.3*

Figure D.4
Demand from MOD Submarine Programmes for Professional Engineers—Combat Systems

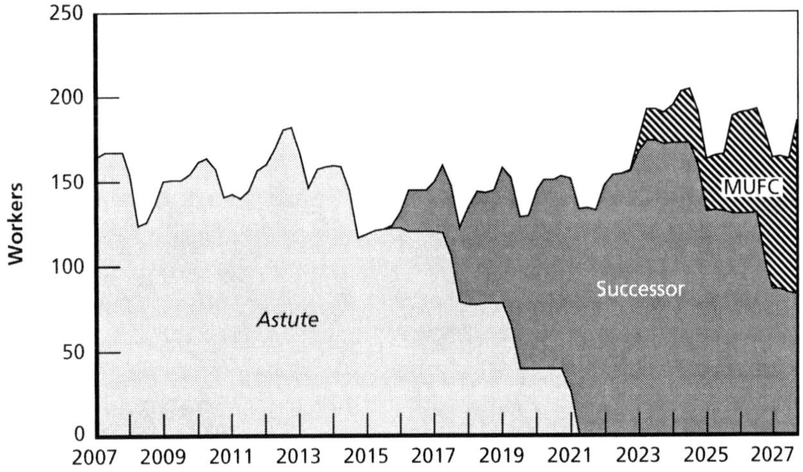

RAND *MG725-D.4*

Figure D.5
Demand from MOD Submarine Programmes for Professional Engineers—Electrical and Control

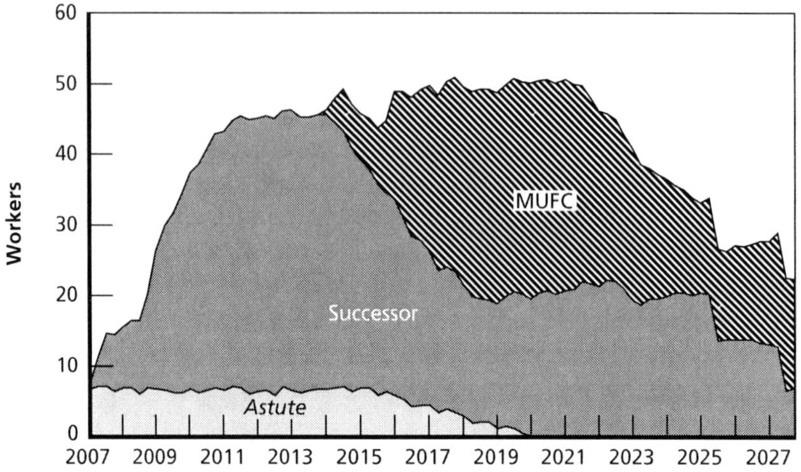

RAND *MG725-D.5*

Figure D.6
Demand from MOD Submarine Programmes for Professional Engineers—Hull/Structural/Arrangements

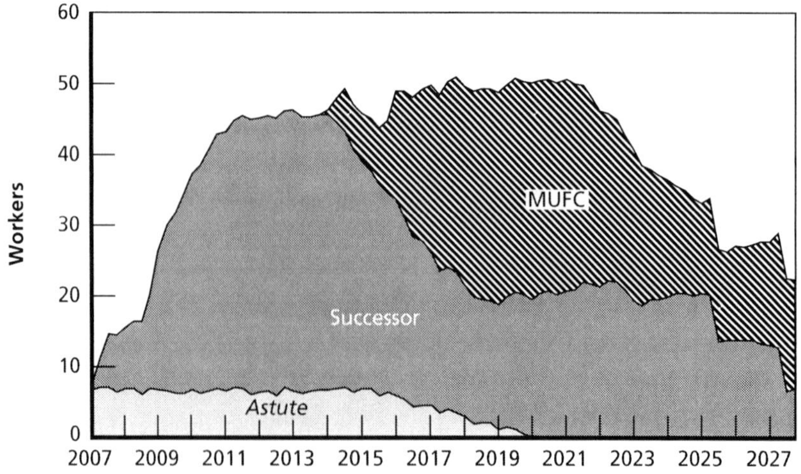

RAND *MG725-D.6*

Figure D.7
Demand from MOD Submarine Programmes for Professional Engineers—Mechanical/Fluids

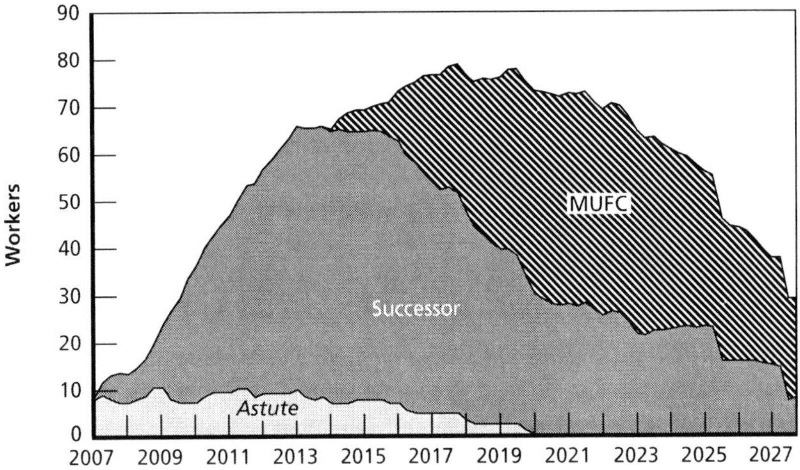

RAND *MG725-D.7*

Figure D.8
Demand from MOD Submarine Programmes for Professional Engineers—Naval Architects

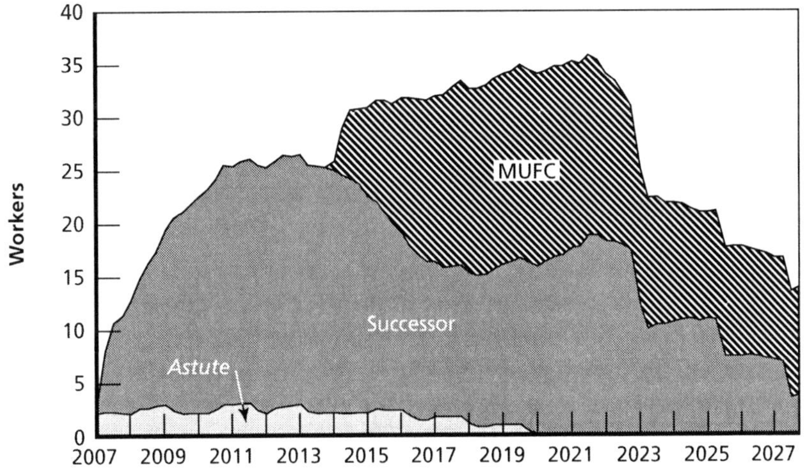

RAND *MG725-D.8*

Figure D.9
Demand from MOD Submarine Programmes for Professional Engineers—Nuclear

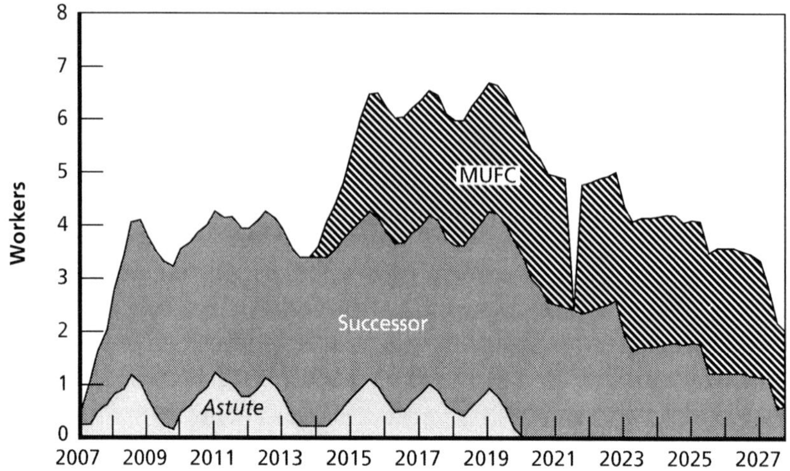

RAND *MG725-D.9*

Figure D.10
Demand from MOD Submarine Programmes for Professional Engineers—Testing and Commissioning

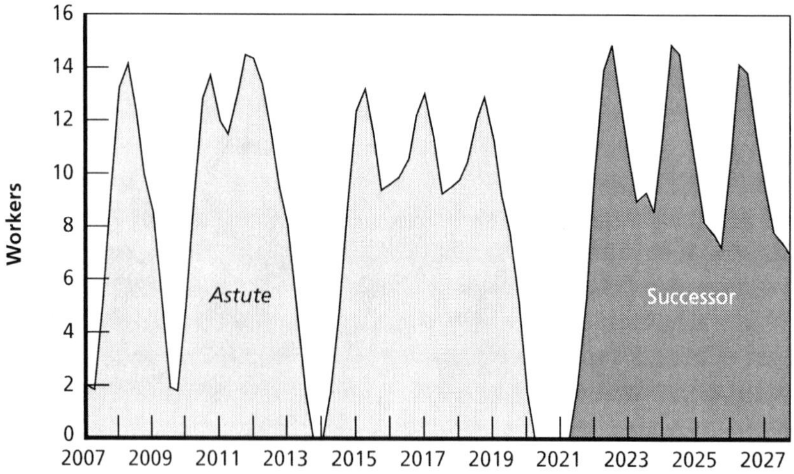

RAND *MG725-D.10*

Figure D.11
Demand from MOD Submarine Programmes for Technical Management—Planning and Production

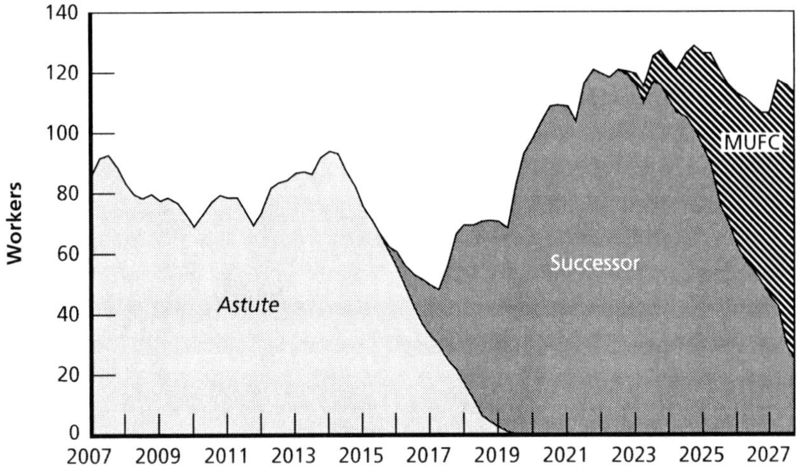

RAND *MG725-D.11*

Figure D.12
Demand from MOD Submarine Programmes for Technical Management—Programme Management

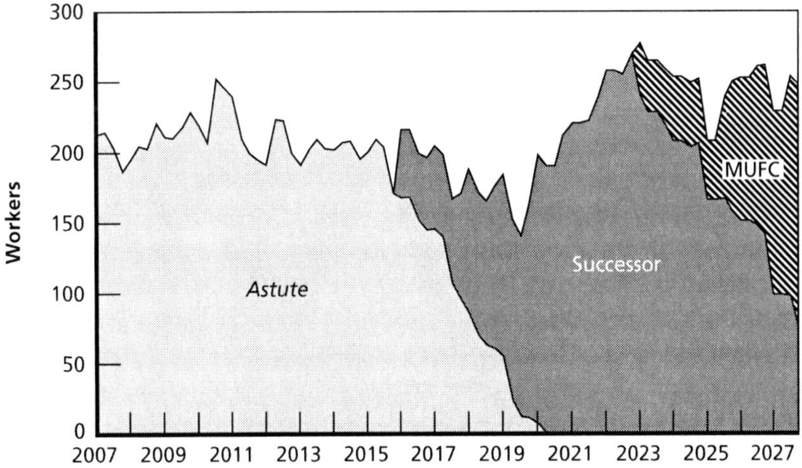

RAND *MG725-D.12*

Figure D.13
Demand from MOD Surface Ship Programmes for Detailed Designers—Electrical and Control

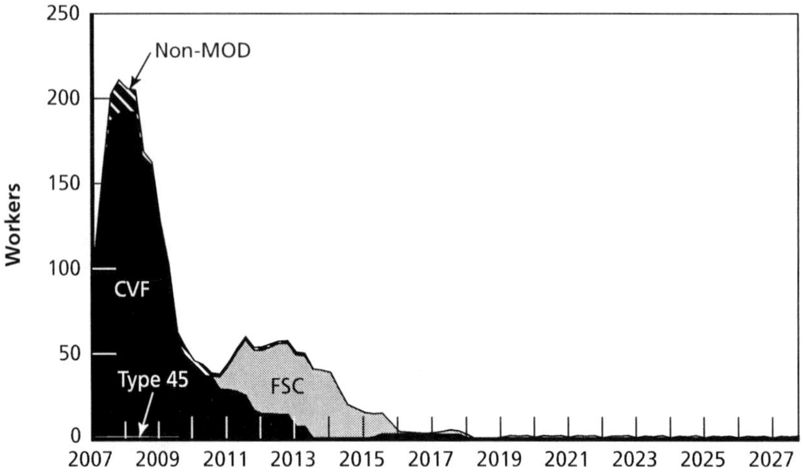

RAND *MG725-D.13*

Figure D.14
Demand from MOD Surface Ship Programmes for Detailed Designers—Mechanical/Fluids

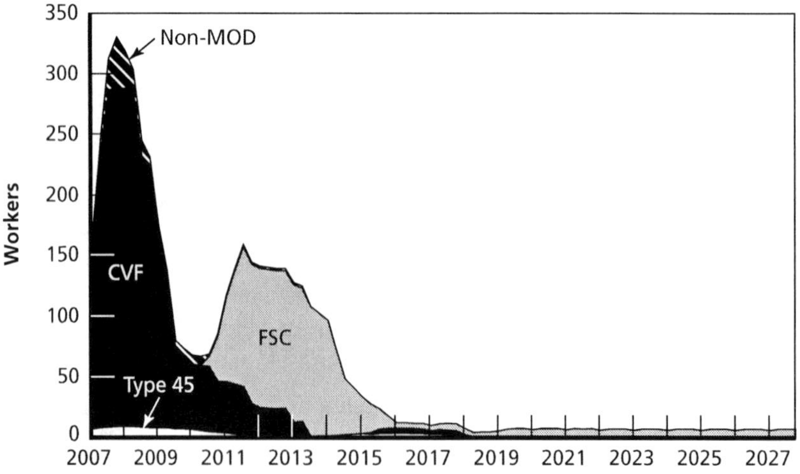

RAND *MG725-D.14*

Figure D.15
Demand from MOD Surface Ship Programmes for Detailed Designers—Hull/Structural/Arrangements

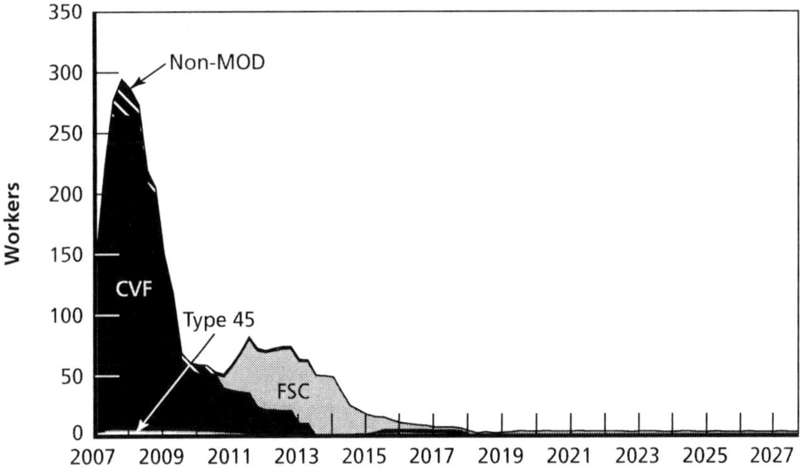

RAND *MG725-D.15*

Figure D.16
Demand from MOD Surface Ship Programmes for Professional Engineers—Combat Systems

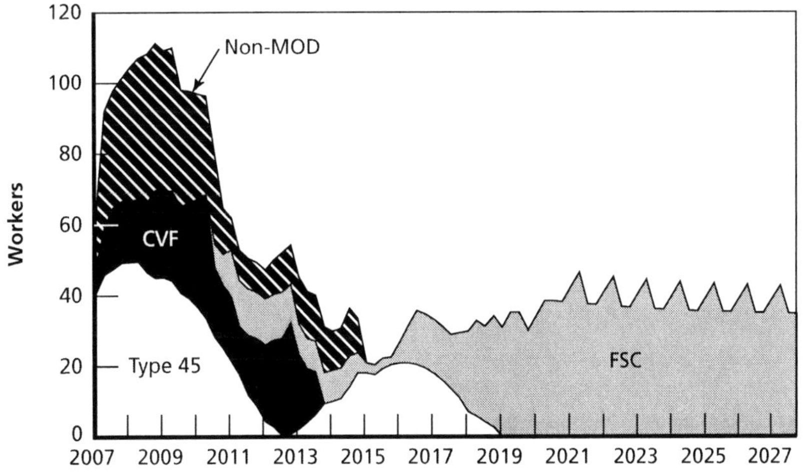

RAND *MG725-D.16*

Figure D.17
Demand from MOD Surface Ship Programmes for Professional Engineers—Electrical and Control

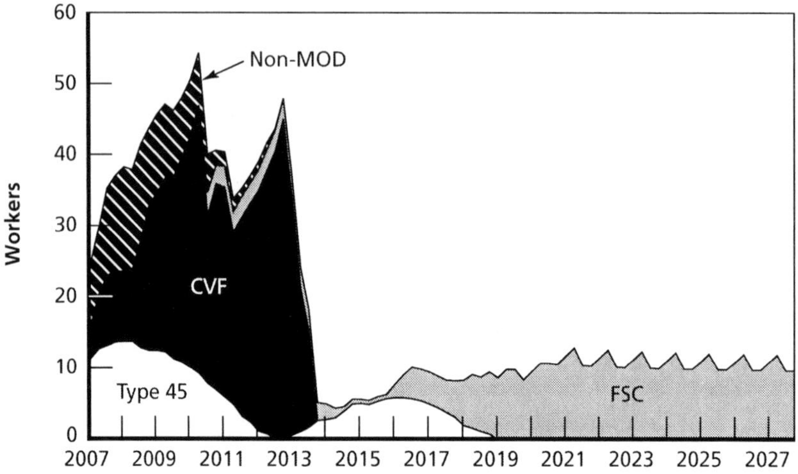

RAND *MG725-D.17*

Figure D.18
Demand from MOD Surface Ship Programmes for Professional Engineers—Hull/Structural/Arrangements

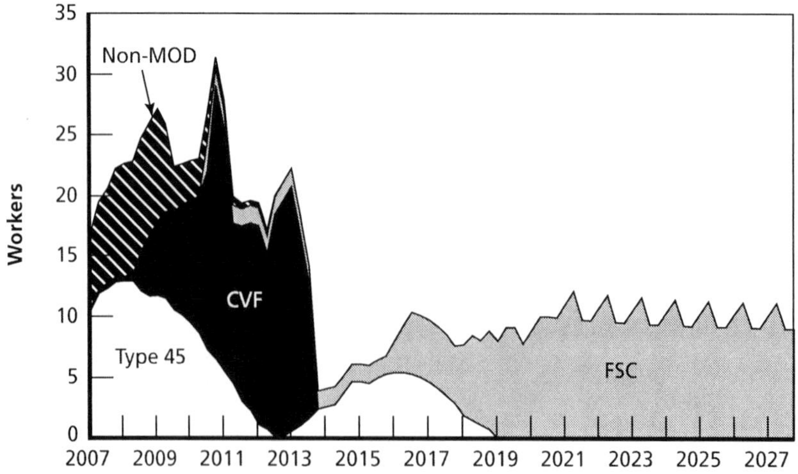

RAND *MG725-D.18*

Figure D.19
Demand from MOD Surface Ship Programmes for Professional Engineers—Mechanical/Fluids

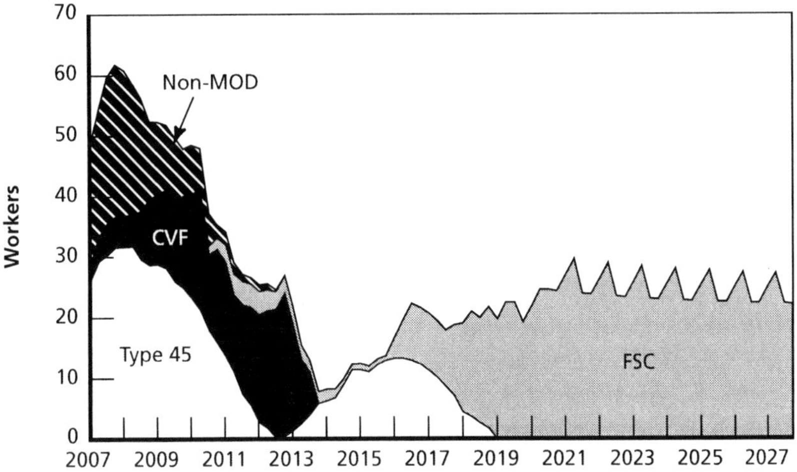

RAND *MG725-D.19*

Figure D.20
Demand from MOD Surface Ship Programmes for Professional Engineers—Naval Architects

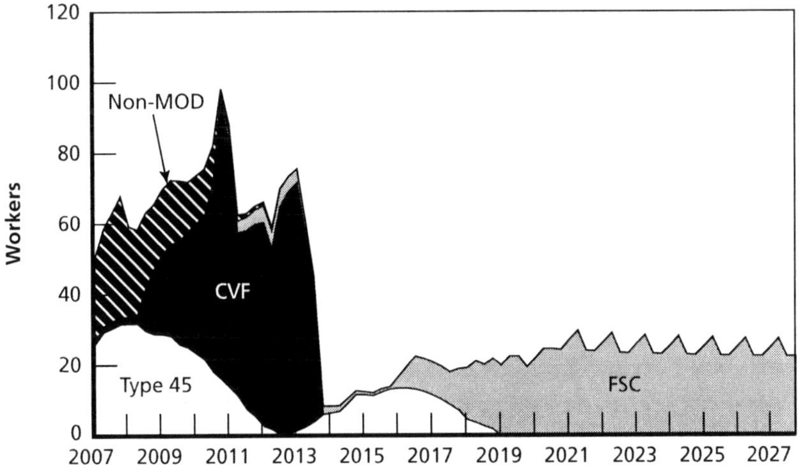

RAND *MG725-D.20*

Figure D.21
Demand from MOD Surface Ship Programmes for Professional Engineers—Testing and Commissioning

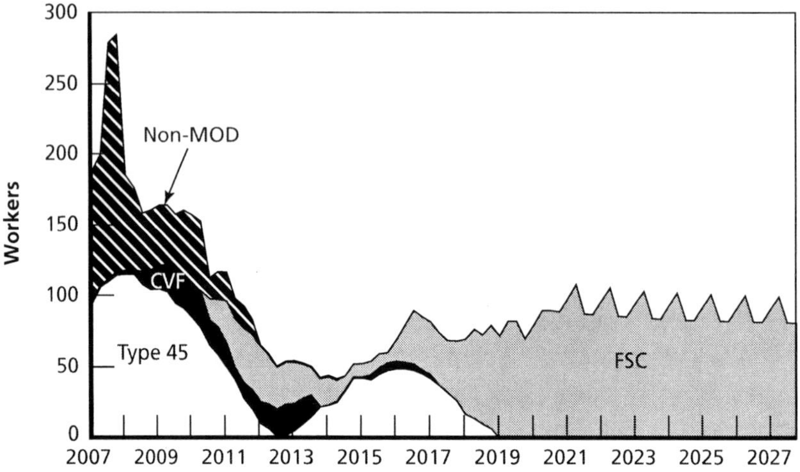

RAND *MG725-D.21*

Figure D.22
Demand from MOD Surface Ship Programmes for Technical Management—Planning and Production

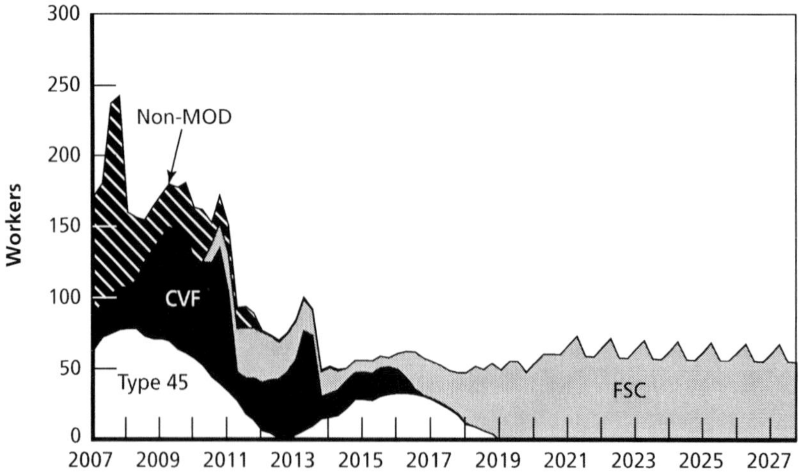

RAND *MG725-D.22*

Figure D.23
Demand from MOD Surface Ship Programmes for Technical Management—Programme Management

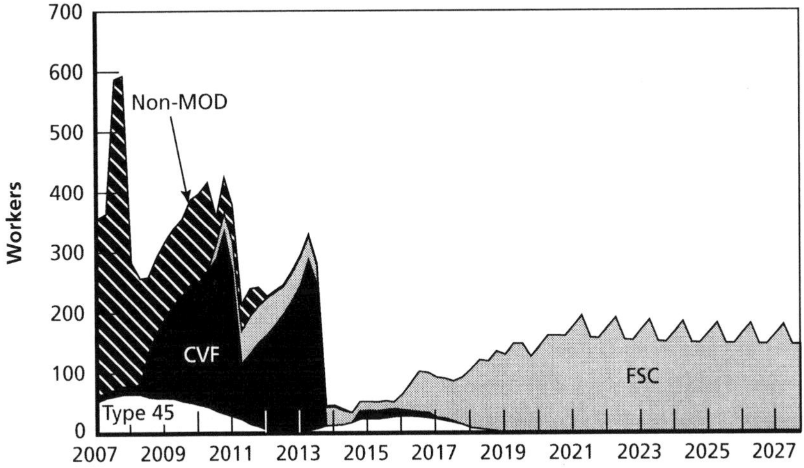

RAND *MG725-D.23*

APPENDIX E

Survey of Shipyards

We sent the following questionnaire to shipbuilders in the spring of 2007. We reproduce it here in its entirety. Note that technical manager skills were grouped with professional engineering skills in the survey.

Maritime Industrial Strategy Study Survey

Introduction

As we discussed during our initial visit(s), the Ministry of Defence (MOD) has asked RAND to conduct a study of key shipbuilding industrial base skills and future issues. As you will remember, the objective of this research is to inform MOD of different core workload options for maintaining shipbuilding design, build, and support in those areas of onshore capability that are considered of UK strategic importance. It will identify the associated critical skills that the core workload should attempt to sustain, specifically in the design and engineering domains. Options to sustain these capabilities and skills will be evaluated. Such options might include potential changes to MOD's planning or new ideas for maintaining critical skills beyond the bounds of current thinking.

Thank you for the data and information that you have provided thus far. We have some further and more specific questions that we have included in the following survey. We are happy to sign a nondisclosure agreement if necessary.

After we have received your completed survey form, we may want to follow up through a phone conversation, email, or another visit.

Please let us know your preference regarding how we should follow up with you for answers to questions or to request clarification on portions of your completed survey.

Thank you again for your assistance with this study.

MOD Contact

Our project monitor is

Jonathan Ackland
MIS Project Team
MOD Abbey Wood
Bristol BS34 8JH

RAND Contacts

If you have any questions or require further clarification, please contact one of the analysts listed below.

Hans Pung
RAND Europe
Milton Road
Cambridge CB4 1YG
+44 (0)1223 273895
Hans_Pung@rand.org

Laurence Smallman
RAND Corporation
1200 South Hayes St.
Arlington, VA 22202
+1 703-413-1100, ext 5198
Laurence_Smallman@rand.org

Persons Completing the Form

Name	Title/Company	Phone Number	Email Address

Instructions

Throughout this survey, please provide data by specific skill category where possible. If data are not available at the specific skill level, please provide them at the detailed designer/professional engineer level. Additionally, please specify which skill categories are included in any "other designer" or "other engineering" categories.

In the survey, we often use the term *technical workforce.* By *technical,* we mean those skills which require design or engineering expertise regardless of where they occur within the procurement life cycle.

We ask for a wide range of data in the survey for three main reasons:

1. to capture information regarding specific technical skills to allow us to better understand current skill availability and experience ("domain knowledge")
2. to capture future skill demand (by phase of MOD programme) to allow us to better understand future requirements for technical skills
3. to capture cost and availability information surrounding build-up and draw-down of technical skills and the overall business base to allow us to better understand the ability of industry, in general, to accommodate differing future design, build, and support plans. This will help us understand what it is both feasible and sustainable for industry to do.

As an aid to our skill-category definitions, we have included the following table, which provides greater detail as to some of the sub-skills that fit into the higher-level skill categories that are the basis of this survey.

Skill Category		Examples of Detailed Skills
Detailed designers	Electrical and control	Electrical system component, electrical analysis, electrical design, power generation
	Mechanical/fluids	Mechanical component; mechanical systems; mechanical design; piping design; heating, ventilation, and air conditioning (HVAC) design; fluid system design; hydraulic system design
	Hull/structural/ arrangements	Structural engineering, structural arrangement, structural design
	Other detailed design	Engineering support, life-cycle support, software engineering, IT support
Professional engineers	Acoustics/signatures/ dynamics	Signature analysis
	Combat systems and integration	Combat system integration, combat system design
	Electrical and control	Electrical system component, electrical analysis, electrical design, power generation
	Mechanical/fluids	Mechanical component, mechanical system, mechanical design, piping design, HVAC design, fluid system design, hydraulic system design
	Naval architecture/ marine	Naval architect, marine engineer, weights analysis, standards
	Planning and production support	Scheduling, Purchasing Support, Component Support
	Hull/structural/ arrangements	Structural engineering, structural arrangement, structural design
	Testing, commissioning, and acceptance	
	Programme management	Programme management, schedule and cost control, estimating
	Safety/environmental	Safety engineers, environmental engineers
	Welding/metallurgy/ materials	
	Propulsion	Shafting and gear design, prime mover analysis, propeller design and analysis

Skill Category		Examples of Detailed Skills
Professional engineers (cont.)	Nuclear specific	Shielding, design, reactor plant design, turbine engineering
	Other engineering	Engineering support, life-cycle support, software engineering, IT support

Technical Workforce Demographics

1. Please provide your company's average number employees in 2006.

Skill Category		Number
Detailed designers	Electrical and control	
	Mechanical (inc. piping, HVAC)	
	Hull/structural/arrangements	
	Other detailed design	
Professional engineers	Acoustics/signatures/dynamics	
	Combat systems and integration	
	Electrical and control	
	Mechanical/fluids	
	Naval architecture/marine	
	Planning and production support	
	Hull/structural/arrangements	
	Testing, commissioning, and acceptance	
	Programme management	
	Safety/environmental	
	Welding/metallurgy/materials	
	Propulsion	
	Nuclear specific (e.g., shielding)	
	Other engineering	

2. Please estimate your company's number of employees in the following categories over the specified years.

Skill Category	1995	2000	2001	2002	2003	2004	2005
Detailed designers							
Professional engineers							

3. Please provide your current workforce age distribution by skill category.

Skill Category		Age (Years)									
		<21	21–25	26–30	31–35	36–40	41–45	46–50	51–55	56–60	>60
Detailed designers	Electrical and control										
	Mechanical (inc. piping, HVAC)										
	Hull/structural/ arrangements										
	Other detailed design										
Professional engineers	Acoustics/signatures/ dynamics										
	Combat systems and integration										
	Electrical and control										
	Mechanical/fluids										
	Naval architecture/ marine										
	Planning and production support										
	Hull/structural/ arrangements										
	Testing, commissioning, and acceptance										

Skill Category		Age (Years)									
		<21	21–25	26–30	31–35	36–40	41–45	46–50	51–55	56–60	>60
Professional engineers (cont.)	Programme management										
	Safety/ environmental										
	Welding/metallurgy/ materials										
	Propulsion										
	Nuclear specific (e.g., shielding)										
	Other engineering										

4. Please provide the current distribution of your workforce by years of experience in the field. *If information is available only for years of employment at your company, please specify this and provide the data in the same format.*

Skill Category		Years of Experience						
		<1	1–2	3–5	6–10	11–20	21–30	>30
Detailed designers	Electrical and control							
	Mechanical (inc. piping, HVAC)							
	Hull/structural/ arrangements							
	Other detailed design							
Professional engineers	Acoustics/signatures/ dynamics							
	Combat systems and integration							
	Electrical and control							
	Mechanical/fluids							

Skill Category		Years of Experience						
		<1	1–2	3–5	6–10	11–20	21–30	>30
Professional engineers (cont.)	Naval architecture/ marine							
	Planning and production support							
	Hull/structural/ arrangements							
	Testing, commissioning, and acceptance							
	Programme management							
	Safety/ environmental							
	Welding/metallurgy/ materials							
	Propulsion							
	Nuclear specific (e.g., shielding)							
	Other engineering							

5. Please both provide the average number of annual permanent hires and annual apprentice intake by skill category over the past five years.

Skill Category		2002–2006 Annual Average	
		Permanent Hires	Apprentice Intake
Detailed designers	Electrical and control		
	Mechanical (inc. piping, HVAC)		
	Hull/structural/arrangements		
	Other detailed design		

Skill Category		2002–2006 Annual Average	
		Permanent Hires	Apprentice Intake
Professional engineers	Acoustics/signatures/dynamics		
	Combat systems and integration		
	Electrical and control		
	Mechanical/fluids		
	Naval architecture/marine		
	Planning and production support		
	Hull/structural/arrangements		
	Testing, commissioning, and acceptance		
	Programme management		
	Safety/environmental		
	Welding/metallurgy/materials		
	Propulsion		
	Nuclear specific (e.g., shielding)		
	Other engineering		

6. Please provide the average age of your workers at the time of their retirement. If this varies by skill category, please indicate this.

7. In the following table, please provide the average number of voluntary departures by skill category over the past five years (i.e., *not* due to layoffs or retirement). What is your typical percentage of attrition *not* including layoffs or retirement?

Skill Category		2002–2006 Average Voluntary Departures	% Turnover Due to Voluntary Departures
Detailed designers	Electrical and control		
	Mechanical (inc. piping, HVAC)		
	Hull/structural/arrangements		
	Other detailed design		
Professional engineers	Acoustics/signatures/dynamics		
	Combat systems and integration		
	Electrical and control		
	Mechanical/fluids		
	Naval architecture/marine		
	Planning and production support		
	Hull/structural/arrangements		
	Testing, commissioning, and acceptance		
	Programme management		
	Safety/environmental		
	Welding/metallurgy/materials		
	Propulsion		
	Nuclear specific (e.g., shielding)		
	Other engineering		

Technical Workforce Planning

8. What is the company strategy for workforce planning when demands change? When work is ramping up, does contract funding constrain the workforce ramp-up rate? When work is falling off, do union restrictions or other factors affect layoff rates?

9. What is the maximum annual growth rate you could *sustain* as a percentage of the workforce? Does this vary by skill? If so, please provide detail.
10. What constrains the workforce ramp-up rate (e.g., productivity, available recruitment pool)?

Technical Workforce Experience, Hiring Pools, and Productivity

11. Please indicate the typical experience level of your new hires as a percent of those hired.

Skill Category		Years				
		<1	1–2	3–4	5–10	>10
Detailed designers	Electrical and control					
	Mechanical (inc. piping, HVAC)					
	Hull/structural/arrangements					
	Other detailed design					
Professional engineers	Acoustics/signatures/dynamics					
	Combat systems and integration					
	Electrical and control					
	Mechanical/fluids					
	Naval architecture/marine					
	Planning and production support					
	Hull/structural/arrangements					
	Testing, commissioning, and acceptance					
	Programme management					
	Safety/environmental					
	Welding/metallurgy/materials					
	Propulsion					
	Nuclear specific (e.g., shielding)					
	Other engineering					

12a. From which sources do you typically recruit new technical workforce?

12b. From what organisations or industries do your experienced technical workforce typically come?

12c. Please describe the typical recruitment pool for your technical workforce (e.g., certain vocational schools, grown within the organisation)

13. Can you identify any existing untapped sources for potential recruitment? Furthermore, to what extent can the industry draw from other industries, and how transferable are these skills?

14a. Are there particular skills or disciplines (e.g. a specific type of engineering) that are in high demand or for which recruiting is difficult? Please explain.

14b. Are there future programmes for which this recruiting difficulty may cause problems or is of concern?

15a. Please estimate your annual training cost (any cost beyond trainee salary) per worker by experience.

	Years								
Skill Category	**<1**	**1**	**2**	**3**	**4**	**5**	**6**	**7**	**>7**
Detailed designers									
Professional engineers									

15b. Are there any skills that have significantly higher training costs? Please describe.

16. Please indicate the relative productivity (percentage relative to the highest-skilled worker) by experience and skill category. We have assumed all workers to be fully productive by 10 years, if this is not the case, please indicate.

Skill Category		Years										
		<1	1	2	3	4	5	6	7	8	9	10
Detailed designers	Electrical and control											100%
	Mechanical (inc. piping, HVAC)											100%
	Hull/structural/ arrangements											100%
	Other detailed design											100%
Professional engineers	Acoustics/signatures/ dynamics											100%
	Combat systems and integration											100%
	Electrical and control											100%
	Mechanical/fluids											100%
	Naval architecture/ marine											100%
	Planning and production support											100%
	Hull/structural/ arrangements											100%
	Testing, commissioning, and acceptance											100%
	Programme management											100%
	Safety/environmental											100%
	Welding/metallurgy/ materials											100%
	Propulsion											100%
	Nuclear specific (e.g., shielding)											100%
	Other engineering											100%

17. How many inexperienced people can an experienced worker mentor? If this varies by skill category, please provide details. We are looking to understand how you use your experienced workforce to train and develop your less experienced workforce.
18. In your experience, what has dictated the shape of your technical workforce labour profiles? Have these profiles typically been symmetrical (or not)? What determines the rate at which you add and subtract people from a specific programme? Does this vary by type or class of ship/submarine? If so, please provide details.
19. Which skills are unique to a specific programme (e.g., submarine specialties) that are not utilised in other types of activity (such as new design, production, and support/repair)? How does this vary by type or class of vessel?

Current and Future Technical Workforce Plans

20. Please provide data concerning your historical and future technical workforce efforts. Please provide data starting with 2006 and going as far into the future as possible. Also, please include activities such as in-service support, export work, research and development efforts, and any other activities that may draw upon your technical workforce resources.

For current and future programmes:

Activity	Name/Description	Start (month/year)	End (month/year)	Type of activity		
				Nonrecurring Design and Engineering (by platform)	Support to Production (by hull)	Support/Repair (by hull)
1						
2						
3						
4						
5						
6						
7						
8						
9						
10						
NOTE: If there are more than 10 activities, please expand the list.						

21. [This question has been removed to protect commercial sensitivity surrounding the future MOD programme.]

Resources Demands

22. For *each* technical workforce activity listed on the "Current and Future Technical Workforce Plans" table (Question 20), please provide the requested information in terms of hours with respect to the workload demand in the shipyard by technical skill (replicate this page as many times as necessary). In the table (on the next page), "quarter 1" refers to the start of each activity.

In addition to the activities listed in Question 20, we would like you to provide technical workforce estimates (if possible) for the activities you selected in Question 21. (If you feel that the estimates in Question 21 are inaccurate, please provide the information using your own estimates and indicate which assumptions you have made.)

Finally, for all in-service support/refit activities, we would like you to provide an additional labour profile estimate for all nontechnical work performed for each support activity.

Activity

Name: ____

Type of Work (e.g., new design, production, upgrade, support):

____

____

____

Number on "Current and Future Workforce Plans" table (Question 20):

____

Skill Category		Quarter															Until	End
		1	2	3	4	5	6	7	8	9	10	11	12	13	14	15		
Detailed designers	Electrical and control																	
	Mechanical (inc. piping, HVAC)																	
	Hull/structural/arrangements																	
	Other detailed design																	
Professional engineers	Acoustics/signatures/dynamics																	
	Combat systems and integration																	
	Electrical and control																	
	Mechanical/fluids																	
	Naval architecture/marine																	
	Planning and production support																	
	Hull/structural/arrangements																	
	Testing, commissioning, and acceptance																	
	Programme management																	
	Safety/Environmental																	
	Welding/metallurgy/materials																	
	Propulsion																	
	Nuclear specific (e.g., shielding)																	
	Other engineering																	
Nontechnical work	All nontechnical labour																	

Changing Technical Skill Requirements

23. It is well understood that using historical data to project future technical activity profiles has certain implications. To better understand how a future technical activity effort may differ from a historical technical activity effort, it is important to understand how a future design may differ. In your opinion, what new skill sets will be required 10 years from now?

24. In your opinion, what existing skill sets will *no longer* be required in 10 years from now or *will be required to a much lesser degree* than at present?

Burden Rate Information

Definition: The term *burden* refers to overhead, general and administrative, and fee/profit costs. This burden is typically proportional to direct hours and billed as a percentage of direct labour hours.

25a. Please provide the average, fully burdened hourly rate for your employees by skill category in 2006 GBP for your technical and design workforce.

Skill Category		Hourly Rate, 2006 Average (£)
Detailed designers	Electrical and control	
	Mechanical (inc. piping, HVAC)	
	Hull/structural/arrangements	
	Other detailed design	
Professional engineers	Acoustics/signatures/dynamics	
	Combat systems and integration	
	Electrical and control	
	Mechanical/fluids	
	Naval architecture/marine	
	Planning and production support	
	Hull/structural/arrangements	

Skill Category		Hourly Rate, 2006 Average (£)
Professional engineers (cont.)	Testing, commissioning, and acceptance	
	Programme management	
	Safety/environmental	
	Welding/metallurgy/materials	
	Propulsion	
	Nuclear specific (e.g., shielding)	
	Other engineering	

25b. What are your standard work hours per year?

26. For your technical workforce, please provide in the table below how burden/overhead changes as a function of the current business base. If you have separate burden rates for different areas or skills, please provide a rate table for each area.

% Change in Business Base	Total Direct Hours	Burden/Overhead Rate (%)	Fully Burdened Rate (£/hr)
20			
10			
0			
–10			
–20			

27. In the above table, what assumptions have you made concerning the fixed burden costs (such as asset depreciation, rent, and facilities maintenance)? Please describe.

____

____

____

Bibliography

"Ahead or Astern: Drayson Ups the Ante on MIS," *Jane's Navy International*, February 6, 2007.

Anderson, Guy, "BAE Systems, VT Joint Venture Surfaces as UK Approves Carrier Construction," *Jane's Defence Industry*, July 25, 2007.

Arena, Mark V., Hans Pung, Cynthia R. Cook, Jefferson P. Marquis, Jessie Riposo, and Gordon T. Lee, *The United Kingdom's Naval Shipbuilding Industrial Base: The Next Fifteen Years*, Santa Monica, Calif.: RAND Corporation, MG-294-MOD, 2005. As of February 4, 2008:
http://www.rand.org/pubs/monographs/MG294/

Arena, Mark V., John F. Schank, and Megan Abbott, *The Shipbuilding and Force Structure Analysis Tool: A User's Guide*, Santa Monica, Calif.: RAND Corporation, MR-1743-NAVY, 2004. As of February 4, 2008:
http://www.rand.org/pubs/monograph_reports/MR1743/

Birkler, John, Denis Rushworth, James Chiesa, Hans Pung, Mark V. Arena, and John F. Schank, *Differences Between Military and Commercial Shipbuilding: Implications for the United Kingdom's Ministry of Defence*, Santa Monica, Calif.: RAND Corporation, MG-236-MOD, 2005. As of February 4, 2008:
http://www.rand.org/pubs/monographs/MG236/

Birkler, John, John F. Schank, Mark V. Arena, Giles K. Smith, and Gordon T. Lee, *The Royal Navy's New Generation Type 45 Destroyer: Acquisition Options and Implications*, Santa Monica, Calif.: RAND Corporation, MR-1486-MOD, 2002. As of February 4, 2008:
http://www.rand.org/pubs/monograph_reports/MR1486/

Critchley, Mike, *British Warships and Auxiliaries*, Cornwall: Maritime Books, 2002.

"European Naval Shipbuilding Industry: Consolidation," *Jane's Navy International*, October 17, 2006.

"Industry Update: Privatisation," *Jane's Navy International*, December 1, 1996.

Jamieson, Alan G., *Ebb Tide in the British Maritime Industries: Change and Adaptation, 1918–1990*, Exeter: University of Exeter Press, 2003.

Johnman, Lewis, and Hugh Murphy, "The Rationalisation of Warship Building in the United Kingdom, 1945–2000," *Journal of Strategic Studies*, Vol. 24, No. 3, September 2001, pp. 107–127.

———, *British Shipbuilding and the State since 1918: A Political Economy of Decline*, Exeter: University of Exeter Press, 2003.

Klinger, Peter, "BAE and VT Drop Bid for Babcock," *The Times*, May 11, 2006, p. 55.

Lamb, Thomas, ed., *Ship Design and Construction*, 2 vols., Jersey City, N.J.: Society of Naval Architects and Marine Engineers, 2003.

Luckhurst, Tim, "The Scuttling of Scotland's Shipping Might," *The Times*, March 11, 2007, p. 2.

Maritime Business Strategies, LLC, "World Shipbuilding Deliveries," April 30, 2005. As of February 4, 2008:
http://www.shipbuildinghistory.com/world/statistics/world.htm

Milner, Mark, "Orders for £3bn Warships Signal a New Era for Naval Defence Industry," *The Guardian*, March 29, 2007. As of June 12, 2007:
http://www.guardian.co.uk/business/2007/mar/29/politics.themilitary

Robertson, David, "BAE and VT Announce Merger as MOD Orders Two New Carriers," *The Times*, July 26, 2007, p. 46.

Schank, John F., Mark V. Arena, Paul DeLuca, Jessie Riposo, Kimberly Curry, Todd Weeks, and James Chiesa, *Sustaining U.S. Nuclear Design Capabilities*, Santa Monica, Calif.: RAND Corporation, MG-608-NAVY, 2007. As of February 4, 2008:
http://www.rand.org/pubs/monographs/MG608/

Schank, John F., Cynthia R. Cook, Robert Murphy, James Chiesa, Hans Pung, and John Birkler, *The United Kingdom's Nuclear Submarine Industrial Base: Ministry of Defense Roles and Required Technical Resources*, Santa Monica, Calif.: RAND Corporation, MG-326/2-MOD, 2005. As of February 4, 2008:
http://www.rand.org/pubs/monographs/MG326.2/

Schank, John F., Jessie Riposo, John Birkler, and James Chiesa, *The United Kingdom's Nuclear Submarine Industrial Base: Sustaining Design and Production Resources*, Santa Monica, Calif.: RAND Corporation, MG-326/1-MOD, 2005. As of February 4, 2008:
http://www.rand.org/pubs/monographs/MG326.1/

Starkey, David J., and Jamieson, Alan G., *Exploiting the Sea: Aspects of Britain's Maritime Economy Since 1870*, Exeter: University of Exeter Press, 1998.

Tomaney, John, Andy Pike, and James Cornford, "Plant Closure and the Local Economy: The Case of Swan Hunter on Tyneside," *Regional Studies*, Vol. 33, No. 5, July 1999, pp. 401–411.

UK Defence Procurement Agency, *Warship Engineering Management Guide*, draft C, MAP 01-020, August 2005.

UK Ministry of Defence, *Defence Industrial Policy*, Ministry of Defense Policy Paper No. 5, October 2002. As of February 4, 2008:
http://www.mod.uk/DefenceInternet/AboutDefence/CorporatePublications/PolicyStrategyandPlanning/PolicyPapers/PolicyPaperNo5DefenceIndustrialPolicy.htm

———, *The Royal Navy Handbook*, London: Conway Maritime Press, 2003.

———, *Defence Industrial Strategy*, Defense White Paper CM 6697, December 2005. As of February 4, 2008:
http://www.mod.uk/DefenceInternet/AboutDefence/CorporatePublications/PolicyStrategyandPlanning/DefenceIndustrialStrategyDefenceWhitePapercm6697.htm